P9-DIJ-288

TOTAL POKER

BY

David Spanier

SIMON AND SCHUSTER : NEW YORK

Designed by Irving Perkins
Manufactured in the United States of America

Library of Congress Cataloging in Publication Data
Spanier, David.
Total poker.
Includes index.
1. Poker. I. Title.
GV1251.S6   795.4'12   76-46391
ISBN 0-671-22441-7

The author is grateful for permission to reproduce the illustrations herein:
    The Inscrutable Poker Face, The Flow of Wisdom, and The Innovation,
from *Webster's Poker Book,* copyright 1925 by H. T. Webster. Copyright
renewed 1952 by Ethel W. Webster. Reprinted by permission of Simon &
Schuster, Inc.
    "Puggy" Pearson, courtesy Wide World Photos.
    Steve McQueen in *The Cincinnati Kid,* from the MGM release *The Cin-
cinnati Kid,* © 1965 Metro-Goldwyn-Mayer, Inc.
    Paul Newman in *The Sting,* courtesy of Universal Pictures.
    The extract from *At Ease: Stories I Tell to Friends* is reprinted by permission
of Doubleday & Company, Inc. © 1967 by Dwight D. Eisenhower.
    The extract from *From Here to Eternity* is reprinted by permission of
Charles Scribner's Sons. © 1951 by James Jones.

FOR MY FATHER
WHO NEVER GAMBLED—
IN HIS MEMORY

Contents

Contents

Preface

The ideal poker book, as someone once advised me, should contain just a few deliberate mistakes. Then when people who read the book sit down later to play with the author, their game will be that little bit off. They will be following his misleading advice and in the process he can take advantage of their bad play.

A nice bluff, to be sure, if a shade overelaborate; so let me say at the start that if there are any misjudgments or mistakes in this book they are not intentional. There is too much to say about poker for an author to want to fabricate anything. In fact one of the things I discovered in writing this book is how deep a subject poker is: one can't really ever get to the boundaries of it; like exploring space, there's always farther to go.

I am indebted to all the writers on poker who have preceded me; to the Dickinson Library of the University of Nevada at Las Vegas and the Library of Congress in Washington for their marvelous facilities; and to several friends and players who have offered constructive comments.

My particular thanks are due to my friend James Rothman, a statistician and market researcher and not a poker player at all, for his indispensable help and advice, and for compiling the tables of odds. Finally, although she doesn't know the first thing about poker and finds a pack of cards almost as mysterious as hieroglyphics, I could never have finished this book without the support, indulgence, and acumen of my wife, Suzy.

. . . the old familiar alchemy, the best drug of them all against this life . . .

—JAMES JONES
From Here to Eternity

CHAPTER ONE

Bluff

Now might I do it pat.
—Hamlet, III, iii.

THE CLASSICAL APPROACH

Bluff is the essence of poker. Yet it is hard to catch on the wing. It can be conceived, at its finest, in the fleeting glimpse of an opportunity, instinctively; or it can be slow and premeditated. It is lurking in every single hand of the game. *Has he or hasn't he got what he says he's got?*

If you have the best standard hand at poker, a royal flush, a hand that can't be beaten, or even if you have four of a kind, from aces on down, there is a reverse problem. You have to try to persuade the other players that you are holding nothing at all, so they will think you are betting a weak hand this time and will call you. But there are 2,598,960 possible hands in a deck of fifty-two cards, and there are only four royal flushes and thirteen fours of a kind; so it follows that virtually all of the time, in close to 100 percent of hands dealt, you will have indifferent or intermediate hands to play on, and you do not *know* if you are best. In all the games I have played in I can recall holding only one straight flush at draw, and maybe a couple at seven card. In the draw hand, no one else had anything at all, and I won merely the ante. There is really no such thing as a good hand at poker, only good situations.

It follows that the art of bluffing lies in recognizing when the *situation* gives you the chance to promote and exploit your hand, whatever it is, into the winning hand.

Remember Herbert Yardley? One of the classic bluffs at

The Inscrutable Poker Face

poker, almost a cliché, occurs at five card draw when you raise the opener, take no cards, and then make the maximum end bet on your pat hand. The others have to figure out: Has he got it or hasn't he? According to Yardley, that most entertaining of poker writers, who describes his espionage and other rascally activities in his memoir, *The Education of a Poker Player* (1957), he ran this bluff forty-one times in a row at the National Press Club in Washington before being caught out. Forty-one times! Was the press so green in those postwar days, Herbert? I ran this bluff two or three times when I first came to Washington, but the boys soon got on to me and started calling.

The National Press Club is a splendid institution indeed because every day of the week there is a game starting around lunchtime and going on through the early afternoon. The bluff went like this: Yardley is sitting at one of the tables looking tight, in fact so tight is he that fellows coming into the room dive for a seat at the other table if they see him sitting there. When it comes around to his deal, and he is therefore last to speak, Herbert, who has been chucking in his hands one after the other with the tireless rapidity of a submachine gun, suddenly raises. Everyone groans. Yardley is in the pot; he must be loaded! And they groan again when he draws no cards and stands pat. Anyone left in checks his hand around to Herbert, who makes the maximum bet. Everyone then folds.

The satisfaction in playing this one as Yardley did and making it stand up is that you can have absolutely *nothing* in your hand and still win a pot handsome enough to pay for the entire session. Take a seven-handed game such as they have at the Press Club with a 25¢ ante, a $2 opener, and a $4 bet after the draw. The pot is opened with one caller and Herbert is sitting last with a hand like Q-10-7-4-2 all mixed up. It's usually too much of a risk to try this gambit with more than two players in the pot, but this time it looks right. Yardley raises.

He reckons that the caller, who has not raised the opener, is marked as weak; he will probably fold rather than call the raise. The opener, who most likely has aces or kings or two highish pairs, will certainly call; he may put Herbert with two higher pairs, though he doesn't know what Yardley's got except that, if he raises, he's loaded. When Herbert, sitting last, takes no cards at all and slides in the maximum bet of $4, the opener quakes: if he has drawn to a pair of aces and not improved, he has no temptation to call; and starting with two pairs, unimproved they look feeble. Is he going to call and lose and have everybody around the table laughing like jackasses because with two lousy pairs he had the temerity to call Yardley with a pat hand?

If the ante is 25¢, two players ahead of Yardley have made the opening bet of $2 and one of them comes along when Yardley raises it to $4, and then, after the draw, Yardley bets a further $4, the pot is worth $15.75. True, Yardley has contributed $8.25 in the process of betting it up, but when the opener, with a derisive snort of protest, throws in his hand, Yardley has made a net gain on the deal of $7.50. With an ante of 25¢ a time, $7.50 will pay for him to play in thirty more pots for nothing, when maybe he can pull the trick again.

The circumstances have got to be right. The bluffer needs a reputation as a tight, no-risk player, and it is easiest if he is dealing and therefore last to speak. Yardley says he had to be sitting last in order to mix his cards in the deck after the hand to prevent anyone seeing what he was up to. But a player as tight as he evidently was could even stage this bluff sitting in second or third seat. The others would reason that if Yardley raises and stands pat sitting under the gun, he's got to have a very powerful hand. Of course, if another player reraises, the bluffer can quietly stack his hand, complaining that he doesn't think two pairs will stand up. It is still a somewhat amazing claim by Yardley that he ran this bluff forty-one times. Surely someone filled a straight or a flush or got curious with three of a kind? But besides being a code breaker and an expert poker player, Yardley was also something of a specialist in tall stories . . .

There are one or two refinements to this basic bluff at draw poker. Personally I prefer to hold two pairs, as a defensive hand, when running it. Suppose you are dealt 8-8-6-6-x. Two small pairs, as Grandpa always told you, is a sucker bet. But the situation looks promising with only two callers ahead and you sitting last. Since the chances of the two low pairs standing up are remote and the odds of filling at 11 to 1 do not match the money in the pot, this is an obvious occasion to raise, in order to knock out one of the callers, and then stand pat. Your end bet may take the pot without opposition, but if someone does "keep you honest" with a pair of aces, you will still hold the winning hand. Then, if you've gotten away with this bluff once or twice, and figure that's about as far as it will go, next time around, after the others have folded, you can spread your winning hand of 8-8-6-6-x face up and inquire sweetly, "What do you guys need to call on?" This will certainly rile anyone who held a better two pairs and insure that when eventually you are dealt a pat hand you will get plenty of callers.

How frequently should a player bluff? George Coffin answers the question, "Bluff often enough to get called about half the time." His theory in *The Poker Game Complete* (1950) is that a player will lose on his called bluffs about what he wins when he buys pots, and so will break even on the strategy. He would actually gain in the long run, says Coffin, because the "free advertising" would encourage calls when he holds big hands.

Well, that ain't necessarily so. Any strategy based on breaking 50-50 is too much like betting on red and black at roulette to make sense at poker. Bluffing, in the crudest form of making a heavy bet to knock out the opposition and win the pot on an otherwise losing hand, is difficult enough to stage successfully. There will be sufficient losing occasions, when the tactic misfires, to provide so-called advertising of loose play, without being deliberately caught out.

Bluff at poker has to be continuously flexible. Of course an element of bluff exists in every sport. In football the quarterback must decide each time he passes the ball how to shake the receiver free of the defense; the defending team must try to read his mind. Or to take an example from contract bridge, a player may make a forcing bid on a weak hand, with no "real value" justification, to stop the opponents from going for rubber, or perhaps to elicit a higher bid from them which they can't make. It is even possible, strange as it may seem, to run a bluff in chess, a game where every move is open. Why else did Bobby Fischer open the sixth game with P-QB4, leading to the Queen's Gambit Declined, in his world title match against Spassky at Reykjavik? He had tested this move only once before in his life in competition, and had never made any secret of his belief that P-K4 was the only sensible opening in chess. In games other than poker, all such maneuvers are designed to throw the opponent off balance; the bluff certainly has relative value at a particular point, but the contest will be decided by the skills of the players at the game over all. By contrast, bluff in poker is an absolute. It is the game itself.

Yet paradoxically there are nights in which one may bluff sparingly, or not at all, throughout the entire session. Why not? The answer: You are winning enough. The very good player will have at the back of his mind a kind of range of what his winnings ought to be in a particular game, given ideal cards. His longer-term objective among friends is to keep the game going and avoid any huge swings that will drive the losers out for good. Playing with strangers in a club is something else again. But in your hometown game, if the cards are running your way and the pots keep coming in, it would be a mistake to be too greedy and win all the money, wouldn't it? One is speaking here of the very good player (the present author, in case anyone wants to know, comes into this category sometimes, and sometimes not). Most of the time, admittedly, one will be trying to win each and every pot on its merits. In that process, the frequency of bluffing will depend on the run of the game. It could happen that you bluff five times in a row and it could happen that you play it close to the chest without risk for a couple of hours.

As well as marking tactical points in the game, bluffing has a strategic value, tracing a line of past bluffs behind and going on into the future. Take the old routine of trying to hit a four flush at draw. A novice drawing a card to four in suit and missing his flush will raise after the draw, thinking he is bluffing, and as sure as God made little green apples he will be seen. The bet is too obvious. But supposing you have hit a flush earlier in the game, *checked* it, and *then* reraised the bettor. He calls and you rake in a hefty pot. Next time you draw to a four flush, you miss it, but still check and reraise. What is the man who got burned last time going to do? Will he see you? Not if he's got two little pairs.

And then again, when the opportunity seems right, you might try the same trick holding two high pairs. On this third time, the man will figure: Last time I let him get away with it. What the hell does he think he's doing to me? All right, I'll see it! And he loses on two pairs. A more subtle player will sniff out what's going on and try to provoke the raiser into revealing his hand. "Come on now, doc, what's going on? Are you four-flushing again or have you gotten lucky this time?" He is trying to catch from your reactions a hint of how strong you really are. He folds all the same, but you have been warned that someone is wise to your game. This player, if he's shrewd, will wait for a chance to turn the tables on you in the same way, a week or maybe a month later. You have your two pairs, draw a card, check, and raise. This time the same man raises you back. He has also drawn just one card. Has he remembered the previous series of hands? You can't put down two high pairs because of the value in the pot. But now you find to your chagrin that he has kept a kicker to three of a kind. You have to know your customer as well as your cards when bluffing.

Bluffing at five card stud is fundamentally different from draw because at stud the cards are open and you know precisely what you are up against. At this game, patterns of play often repeat themselves, and if someone takes your measure he can beat a tattoo on you.

Here's an example: Jack the bear, a strong, attacking player, leading the betting against me was showing (?)-9-A and I was sitting on (K)-10-K. He bet and I raised him to test the water, indicating a pair of kings or at least tens. With no hesitation he reraised. He is saying loud and clear that he has paired his aces. What do you do? Unless he's a notorious bluffer, you fold. It's too expensive trying to prove your kings are better. Then a couple of hands later it happened again. The same player is showing an ace over my paired kings and bets. What do you do this time around? Can he really have it twice running? Sitting on (K)-10-K, it is hard to throw the hand away. He *could* be bluffing, remembering how he saw me off last time; or he could easily have it. What is more, I rather liked the way this fellow played. Every time he was dealt an ace face up, he would give a little grin as he peeped at his hole card and announce: "One of these days I'm gonna look down here and I'm gonna find another li'l ol' . . . by God!" If there is no firm evidence either way, the decision has to be taken on the basis of the money on the table. If you are well ahead and can afford a speculation, you can call the bet; if you are playing table stakes and don't have too much money in front of

you, you can even raise the bet back and force *him* to decide,
if he hasn't got aces, whether you've really got kings. But if he
is well ahead of the game and playing confidently, a known
tight player, he's probably got the aces, and you fold. And
then when he derisively flips over a queen in the hole (as he
did on this coup), you keep your temper, observing dourly,
"Your ace was better than my king all the time."

These either/or situations, typical of five card, are difficult
to read. I got burned that way the first time I was invited to
play in the Tuesday night game at the Army and Navy Club
in Washington. A square and stately building on Farragut
Square, where officers and their ladies take dinner and remi-
nisce about old times, the club sports a handsome cardroom
on the top floor. The game usually alternated between five
card stud and draw, or seven card, with limit raises of $30. On
this first evening when I appeared, suitably scrubbed and polite, I found myself late in the evening in a largish pot at five
card stud, opposing a peppery old retired officer who was
showing an ace. I had an ace in the hole and on the fifth card
I made a pair of jacks, showing (A)-J-x-x-J. I checked. The
colonel with (?)-A-x-x-x bet $30 at me, ignoring my jacks, so
I raised him back, signifying two pairs or even three of a kind.
I thought it was a damn good bet, myself, but the colonel,
leading the cavalry charge at full tilt, raised me again. Out of
shame more than curiosity I called, and found his aces wired.
No one said a word. Smarting from this self-imposed wound,
I ended up a loser, and I could sense that the table thought I
would never survive in this group. The following week when
the situation was reversed I took my revenge. This time I had
aces wired, and after some fairly cautious betting in which I
did not improve, I was left in with the colonel showing (?)-K-
x-x-x. I checked my aces and without any hesitation he raised.
After a momentary pause to savor the situation, I reraised and
of course he called. It was the previous pattern of play that

influenced the way the hand went. There was a slight, barely audible sigh from around the table as I pulled in the pot. And I won at that gathering seven weeks on the trot before I lost a second time.

Many situations at five card stud leave you holding the whip hand. Accordingly, one of the main bluffs is to try to convince the opposition, when you know you have a lock, that in fact you are weak. You can check, look worried, bet small, or do anything else to encourage them to get their feet wet. One of the best descriptions of poker ever written, specifically about being taken for a ride at five card stud, is in James Jones's novel *From Here to Eternity*, his saga of Army life in Hawaii in the days before Pearl Harbor. It's payday and the soldiers are lining up for their month's pay, those paltry few dollars which will have gone on drink and women long before the next day's reveille is sounded. But first comes the action in the motor sheds, where the men try to play up their pay into a decent-sized stake. Prewitt, the "hero" of the story, after painstakingly working up his $12 to the $20 needed for sitting in at the poker tables, finds a seat open. He wants to win just two pots and then quit, and he wins the first one right away, luckily drawing a third jack to his jacks wired. But then "the old familiar alchemy" gets to him.

It was true poker, hard monotonous unthrilling, and he truly "loved it . . . But before the big win he was just waiting for to quit on came they caught him, they caught him good.

"He had tens backed up, a good hand. On the fourth card he drew another. On the same card Warden paired kings showing. Warden checked to the tens. Prew was cautious, they were not *trying* to play dirty poker in this game but with this much on the table anything went. Warden might have trips and he was not being sucked in, he was not that green. When the bet had checked clear around to him he raised lightly, very lightly, just a touch, a feeler, a protection bet he could afford to abandon and lose. Three men dropped out right away. Only O'Hayer and Warden called, finally. O'Hayer obviously had an ace paired to his holecard and was willing to pay for the chance to catch the third. O'Hayer was a percentage man, twenty percentage man, O'Hayer. And Warden who thought quite a while before he called looked at his holecard twice and then he almost didn't call, so he had no trips.

On the last card O'Hayer missed his ace and dropped out, indifferently. . . . Warden with his kings still high checked it to Prew, and Prew felt a salve of relief grease over him for sure now Warden had no trips. Warden had two pair and hoped the kings would nose him out since O'Hayer had two bullets. Well, if he wanted to see them he could by god pay for seeing them, like everybody else, and Prew bet twenty-five, figuring to milk the last drop out of him, figuring he had this one cinched, figuring The Warden for his lousy pair to brace his kings. It was a legitimate bet; Warden had checked his kings twice when they were high. Warden raised him sixty dollars."

Poor old Prew. How could he have fallen for it when he knew all the time, read it exactly, in fact, what was going on? The answer to that is that Prew, though a finer and truer soldier than all the other men on the base, was a loser, a loser in poker as in life. When Warden looked at his hole card a first and then a second time and then almost didn't call, he gave his hand away. He was trying to bluff that he *didn't* have the third king.

Warden	(?)	K x K
O'Hayer	(?)	x x A
Prew	(10)	10 x 10

If Warden bets out on the fourth card, O'Hayer will certainly
fold his aces and Prew will just call. Far better to check: the
odds against three kings being outdrawn on the fifth card are
so long that Warden can easily take that risk, meanwhile en-
couraging the tens to bet the hand for him. Prew bet just a
touch, his first mistake. Of course Warden is not going to raise
it back: he is deliberately attempting to give the impression
that he has only two pairs. Prew should have checked because
he couldn't afford to be wrong about this one, with his limited
amount of money. If he had had $1,000 behind him it would
be different. In that case he might have bet the pot, and if
Warden raised him back, he could have folded without feeling
too badly about it. There is always the next hand coming up.

Prew's second mistake was betting $25 after the last card.
If Warden decided that he wants to check his hand again, because he had only kings up and feared three tens, let him
check it. If that is so, Prew's bet of $25 will only be called, at
best another $25. Whereas if Warden has trip kings all the
time, he is going to sock it back to Prew and the investment of
$25 is going to cost him far more than he stands to win.
Doesn't everyone know that at five card stud you never (well
almost never) bet into a possibly stronger hand, certainly not
when the top sergeant is in there showing a big fat king right
from the start?

Prew's third mistake was the only one that was serious, indeed it was fatal. He called the $60 reraise. ". . . he made as
if to drop out, but he knew he had to call. There was too much
of his money in this pot, which was a big one, to chance a
bluff." The hand cost him $200 even. It is easy enough to criti-
cize plays like this (which we all make) in the clear light of
reason away from the emotion of the table. Still, the final $60,
really the final $85, was absolutely money down the drain and
Prew knew it. Warden's bluff was based on self-restraint. If he
had bet the three kings out on the fourth card he might have

gotten called by Prew in any case; but it was much more likely that a nervous player, worried about his stack, would have hesitated and backed down. In that case the winning pot would have been worth only half as much.

Restraint, as Warden demonstrated, is a useful quality. If courage is the fuel of bluff, restraint is the gearshift. Take low-ball, which, like five card stud, has clearly defined best hands. In draw low, A-2-3-4-6 (or A-2-3-4-5 if the wheel works) is unbeatable, while an eight low is usually a winning hand. Sitting under the gun, it is normally a sound tactic to raise on a nine or ten low, or even a court card, to drive the opposition out; but it is better tactics to show restraint in checking a strong hand like a good eight or pat seven. If someone else bets after you, you can come back at him, getting maximum impact for your raise, or throw the top card and go for the wheel. And when, after drawing no cards, your final bet is seen and you win the pot, you will have set up a classic bluff for next time: standing pat on a bust and then raising the opener. Unlike high draw, where it is an enormous advantage to be sitting last, the sooner you can get your raise in at low, the better. Once players know you are inclined to hold back on good hands, they will be very chary of seeing you again. A friend of mine in Washington, much given to checking and raising, was dealt four sixes in a low draw hand and was so angry he took every raise and stood pat. I was left in the pot with him, sniffing out that something funny was going on. As I pondered calling the final bet on my good 8-7, my opponent turned his hand toward me, showing just the bottom six. He knew, of course, no matter what, that I couldn't have a six in my hand. "Mine's just a bad six," he said calmly. "How good is your six?" I folded.

The stock image of bluffing at poker is of gunslingers in ten-gallon hats raising and reraising the pot until the table is piled high with silver and bank notes, whereupon one of the two cowboys calls the final bet, and the hero flips over his hole card to show the vital card that makes his winning straight flush. Remember *The Cincinnati Kid?* This was a cool, tight little story (1963) by Richard Jessup of how a young pro, the Kid, stalked and challenged and finally lost to Lancey Howard ("the Man")—" 'all the squares that play cards know he's the Man and invite him to sit in on their little square games and lose to him, jus' so they can say they played with him, see?'" The showdown turned on a somewhat incredible hand of five card stud, illustrating the interaction between courage and restraint.

On the third card the Kid has   (Q ♥) 10 ♣ 10 ♦
Against Lancey's   (?)   7 ♥ 8 ♥

The Kid bet $500 to steal a routine pot of $250. Lancey raised him $300. Now what kind of bet is that? At stud, no one can conceivably bet that way in the hope of catching a straight or a flush. The odds are just too long, too expensive. Of course if you can stick around cheaply, that's something else. Accordingly, the Kid immediately raised him back $2,000, just over the size of the pot. Correct! What can Lancey have even to bluff on? If he's bluffing an ace or a low pair, sevens or eights, so that if he catches another pair showing he can beat the tens, he's in a very unfavorable odds-to-money situation. If he has another heart, even a three straight flush with the 6 ♥ or the 9 ♥, he has a lo-o-ong way to go, especially with two of the tens—and possibly a third, even the 10 ♥—out in the Kid's hand already. It's no kind of bluff to raise $300, when all such a bet does is invite a knockout by the reraise. But Lancey calls the $2,000.

There's no justification, the call just isn't on, and at this point, clearly enough, the demands of a good story take precedence over good poker. With just under $6,000 in the pot, the fourth card is dealt, and Lancey is fantastically lucky. The hands now show:

The Kid	(Q ♥) 10♣ 10♦ Q ♦
Lancey	(?) 7 ♥ 8 ♥ 10 ♥

Now Lancey has a chance to hit. To be precise, if he has the J ♥ in the hole, there are eight hearts to give him a flush (the Kid's hole card is a heart, remember), including the nine for a straight flush, and the three other nines to give him a straight, a total of eleven cards. (Only three cards will help the Kid: the case ten or either of the two queens will give him a full house. But as against that, he doesn't *need* help; he is winning already.) Lancey's chances of improving are 11 out of 44, the number of cards left in the deck, odds of 3 to 1; in fact, slightly over this, since the Kid might get a full house to beat Lancey's straight or flush. The Kid will win if Lancey is dealt any of the other thirty-three cards. The Kid's chances of winning, taking into account his chance of hitting his full house, are actually 36 out of 44, or 4 out of 5.

At this point, the Kid bets $1,000. Not a good move. On the money odds, he is now giving Lancey 7 to 1, $7,000 in the pot for a $1,000 call on his 3 to 1 chance, which is indeed "value." He must read Lancey for a heart in the hole, possibly the ace, probably the nine. So he should make Lancey pay for the chance of his flush, and bet the pot at him, forcing Lancey to put his whole stack in. To have to put up $6,000 to win $12,000 is not an attractive bet in that situation, with the Kid already looking down his throat with the winning hand, as Lancey would know only too well. But the Kid's come-on bet gives Lancey his chance on a plate: " 'A thousand is a cheap enough ride,' Lancey said, his voice easing back onto a friendly quality that had characterized his manner early in the game. He picked up his hundreds and counted off ten bills from the stack. 'One thousand for the call,' he said." And the last card gives him the elusive 9 ♥, the one card that he wants from the forty-four left in the deck.

| The Kid | (Q ♥) 10 ♣ 10 ♦ Q ♦ Q ♠ |
| Lancey | (J ♥) 7 ♥ 8 ♥ 10 ♥ 9 ♥ |

The Kid has hit his full house, but that is irrelevant now. The mathematics is over. If Lancey has been playing a wild hand, up in the empyrean, on a hunch and a prayer, then the Kid should check. Maybe Lancey has a miracle 6 ♥ or J ♥ in the hole. Why bet into that chance? If Lancey has got it, he will raise the Kid out of his seat, whereas if he hasn't got a straight or a flush, he's not even going to call the bet. The Kid has some $1,400 left, so what's a lousy extra $1,400 either way? As it is, Lancey calls at once and raises all he has left in front of him, $4,000. If the Kid had checked the last bet, he could have sat back and considered, when Lancey set himself in with his remaining $5,000, whether his full house was beaten or not. Of course the Kid calls (Lancey has already told him he will accept his marker for the bet), and Lancey turns over the J ♥ for his straight flush. The Kid has to call, not just for the money but because he has to *know*, he couldn't live with himself for the rest of his life not knowing. And this illustrates a cardinal point about bluffing, which is that, at the end, in the very big hands anyway, you are almost certainly going to be seen. The guys in the button-down shirts, like the guys in the ten-gallon hats, are just too curious. They may fold against a bluff when they hold a moderate hand, but if a man has some kind of a poker hand, certainly anything as high as a full house, he is simply not going to believe he is beaten, however big his adversary's final bet.

The Kid did one very sensible thing at that stage. He did not borrow money to go on playing, when his judgment had been shot to hell. He got up from the table and cleaned up in the bathroom, and he and Lancey shook hands like gentlemen and made small talk about the game, about how tired they both were and what a good game it was, the room was cleared out and Lancey said goodbye. The Kid got drunk and stayed drunk, left the poker scene altogether and, supported by his girl friend (the little lady is a saint, but see Chapter Seven for that story), gradually worked it out of his system and stopped drinking. After a time he was ready to go back to the game, staked by his girl friend's earnings as a waitress. "He came on strong and in three days, it was as if he had never been away . . ." You may bluff or you may be bluffed, but there's always next week's game.

In assessing any given play, a balance has to be struck between instinct and mathematics. They may tilt one way and then the other in the course of a single hand. In the final coup with Lancey, the Cincinnati Kid got the balance upset. He allowed his calculation of the chances to be overridden midway through the hand by overconfidence. "He wanted Lancey to turn over his cards and show how foolish he had been." Whereas if he had bet it up and Lancey had still called, despite all that money, and had then drawn out, the Kid would have suffered no disgrace. Everyone would have said Lancey was a lucky sonofabitch. Anyone can draw out, even against the odds.

A RINGSIDE SEAT

One of the supreme instances in modern sport of bluff being carried through with total success was demonstrated, for all the world to see, in the blood-and-thunder atmosphere of a world heavyweight fight. That kind of contest may seem a long way removed from colored pasteboards skimming lightly across the card table; nevertheless, boxing offers some revealing analogies with bluff in poker.

For a start, one does not usually think of boxing as a *rational* activity, a sport where reason plays a very big part, if any at all. But at the highest level of skill, mind is often considerably more powerful than matter. Just how much so is brought out by the career of the boxer whom most people might think of as the least reasonable and most emotional of all contemporary fighters. But that just shows how Muhammad Ali manages to bluff the public a lot of the time, as well as his opponents.

Title fights can be seen preeminently as contests of minds and wills, where each boxer is seeking to outthink or outguess his opponent. The punches each man can throw, the boxers' respective physiques, are assumed to be more or less comparable, just as their weights are broadly equal. It is not these factors in themselves that are likely to decide the outcome, any more than the cards dealt at poker decide who wins and who loses.

Rather it is the *use* made of his technique, the mental effort applied, which determines how a boxer reads his opponent, his tactics in carrying the fight forward, and his strategy in bringing it to an end. These, in short, determine whether a man is a winner or a loser, and on this score Ali is one of the most subtle fighters the game has ever produced.

That is the verdict of another world champion, the gifted Puerto Rican José Torres. According to Torres, elaborating his thesis in a round-by-round analysis of Ali's early fights in . . . *Sting Like a Bee* (1971), fighters always "lie" to deceive their opponents. Champions and good fighters are champions and good fighters because they can *lie* better than the others.

What Torres is really talking about is bluffing. Substituting "bluff" for "lie," the parallel with poker becomes quite striking: "A feint is an outright bluff. You *make believe* you're going to hit your opponent in one place, he covers the spot and your punch lands on the other side." That is a straightforward bluff, so to speak. "A left hook off the jab is a classy bluff.

You're converting an I into an L." That is a bluff conceived in mid-flight, as the opportunity offers. "Making openings is starting a conversation with a guy, so another guy (your other hand) can come and hit him with a baseball bat." That is the continuous process of disguising your intentions.

Yes . . . but lying, or bluffing, goes much further than that. Ali's bluffing was not confined merely to disguising his punches, making what looked like a jab turn into a left hook. That's elementary technique, which any poker player might adopt. The originality of Ali's bluffing was extended and elaborated to cover his total approach to fighting. His predictions, his "lip," his way of riling or upsetting his opponents, were activities of the mind and personality that bluffed his opponents, so that they frequently reacted in the wrong way. Often they were "psyched out" before they ever climbed into the ring, and his verbal banderillas didn't stop even then.

Perhaps all this activity aimed at upsetting his opponents went too far, for there was a time when he overdid it and in effect started bluffing himself by predicting the rounds when his fights would end. (Poker players can't, wouldn't normally want to go so far as that.) But words alone don't score knockouts. And according to the boxing experts, Ali did not have the power, he did not have the punches, he did not even have the moves of the greatest champions. Yet he became the supreme fighter of his day, perhaps the outstanding champion in the history of the sport to date. How so?

The explanation is simple, says Torres. Ali had another power that the greatest fighters never had (in such degree, presumably): he outthought his opponents, as a poker player would—nothing to do, by the way, with intelligence as measured by IQ tests. When the young Clay was called up for military service, he flunked his preinduction mental tests. Faced with questions like "A vendor was selling apples for $10 a basket: how much would you pay for a dozen baskets if one-third of the apples had been removed from each of the baskets?" the twenty-two-year-old Clay hadn't the faintest idea about the answer. He was classified 1-Y, and it was not until the Army had drastically lowered its pass mark two years later that he was reclassified 1-A.

In the ring, Ali's tactics were based on a particular talent, which the best poker players could be said to share: he was very seldom hit. He moved fast. Not getting hit is the most important quality for a fighter to learn; it presents minimum opportunity to the opponent and opens the way for counterattack. For when you know you are not going to get hit, two other instincts are sharpened and brought into play: the sense of anticipation and a feeling of confidence. As Torres puts it, not getting hit improves a man's desire, confidence builds up his will; desire and confidence feed the intelligence, the ability to think fast and achieve the right body-mind coordination. Just as in poker, a player frightened of being hit, of losing big, will certainly perform poorly. Whereas the player who *knows* he is not going to get hurt—he may be hit, he may lose hands, but his reflexes and judgment are going to keep him out of serious trouble—that player has an enormous advantage.

That brings us to the world title match between Ali and George Foreman in Kinshasa in October 1974. Foreman, as everyone knew, was a b-i-i-i-g puncher. He had never been defeated and in his thirty-eight fights he had scored ten knockouts in the first round, eleven in the second, and ten in the third and fourth rounds—a fantastic record. Ali, as everyone also knew, did not have a big punch. How was he going to overcome Foreman, the destroyer of Joe Frazier, whom Ali had fought twice, losing the first match and winning the second only on points, both fights going the distance. The unstoppable power of Foreman's punching had led the bookmakers to install him as odds-on favorite (and I must confess persuaded me to take those miserable odds and put my wager on the wrong man; fortunately I was playing poker that night and got my stake back).

The almost universal expectation was that Ali, in this supreme test of his career, would try to *dance* his way out of trouble, keep moving, keep his distance, let his opponent come to him and hope to counterpunch when the opportunity offered.

Now, what was the true, the complete, the inspired bluff in this situation?

A clue was given. Ali was asked by a reporter before the fight: If you were to advise Foreman how to fight you, what would you tell him? The answer: *Lay back and wait.* The exact opposite of the conventional wisdom!

Even then, Ali, with typical gusto, observed that he would convert this to his own advantage, but it is clear why the advice was sound. For Foreman to stand in the center of the ring and tempt his challenger to come to him would have reversed all the expectations of how he intended to carry the fight, would have forced Ali to change his tactics and his prearranged plans. Bluff always lies in the unexpected.

Knowing in advance what Foreman was going to do, Ali reversed the play. Instead of seeking to dance his way out of getting hit, he stood there and took the punches. This master bluff was not exactly prearranged, settled in advance, though trainer Angelo Dundee did nip around the ring just before the fight and without so much as a by-your-leave loosened all the ropes. The bluff arose from the tactical situation in the fight itself. Ali didn't just lay back; he dodged and wove outside the punches, deflected and blocked the punches. The bluff (but based on highly developed technique and clever use of the ropes) was that Foreman couldn't hurt him *even when he stood still.*

But how was the fight to be won? Not getting hit is one thing, but it is aggressive action, after all, that wins the day, in poker as in anything else.

It was manager Cus D'Amato's theory, which Torres had learned and Ali had absorbed, that if a fighter sees a punch coming, he can register it, communicate its force to his body and reduce its impact, maintaining his consciousness and control. This is an integral and, indeed, natural part of the theory that boxing is a contest of wills, not abilities, which, as we have said, are presumed to be roughly equal.

By contrast, when the man getting hit doesn't see the punch, his brain can't prepare him to receive the impact of the blow, his eyes can't send the message back to the part of his body that would take the shock. He loses control, not so much because of the force of the punch but because he is unprepared for it. Ali did not have a big punch. Typically, he won his fights by a whole flurry of punches, a rapid-fire combination, in which it was not the force itself that counted, but the cumulative disorientation of his opponent. "The sudden overloading of the victim's message center produces that inrush of confusion known as coma," as Norman Mailer has put it. Fortunately, poker is not so brutal, but it is the cumulative effect of accurate play—never showing your hole cards, always betting it up, wit and verbal gymnastics exercized to the right degree, continually pressing, pressing, pressing—that in the hardest-fought games wears down the opposition and puts you ahead on the night.

In the fight in Kinshasa, Ali lay back on the ropes and Foreman ran into the punches. It was not Ali's last right cross that put Foreman down; it was the impact of all the punches combined that produced the final knockout, and those individual punches were themselves close consecutive links in the overall build-up of the fight.

In poker terms, no need to hold the four aces pat. Small hands, like aces up beating kings up, are going to win a whole bucket of money if the coup is delivered with the right timing. Bluff is a matter of a player disorienting the other players at the table, getting them scurrying every which way in response to his pressures, and then making the accurate bet or raise, measured to the moment, which catches them off balance and wins the big one. Shazam!

An Academic View

Surprisingly enough, bluff in poker has been the subject of some extremely abstruse academic studies. The reason is that the game as a system has measurable limits and possibilities. As such, poker (albeit in a simplified form) was found to be a useful model in that somewhat rarefied branch of higher mathematics known as game theory.

Game theory is a study of the decision-making process, taking into account the actions of someone whose decisions may be in conflict with yours. Obviously this applies to games of all kinds, and it surfaces in economics in the form of bargaining and in international relations in the form of diplomacy.

The seminal work is contained in Von Neumann and Morgenstern's *The Theory of Games and Economic Behavior* (1944). John von Neumann was one of the most original mathematicians of our times, the exemplar of that breed of Mittel-European academics whose creative powers reached their fulfillment in the United States. He invented computer programming; he developed the first theory of self-reproducing machines; he redefined the theory of numbers; he helped develop the H-bomb. One of his most striking ideas, according to the *Encyclopaedia Britannica* (1974), was to dye the polar ice caps and so decrease the amount of energy they would reflect; the result would warm the earth enough to make the climate of Iceland resemble that of Hawaii! He also took an interest in poker, though not, I fear, as a player.

What his celebrated treatise on games and economic behavior is concerned with is the strategy of games, and, in particular, the question: What is the best strategy to adopt when the person you are playing against can adopt a strategy that depends on the line you have taken?

For a start, let's take a simple example. When your young son plays chess with you, he will move a piece to attack your undefended piece in the hope that you don't "see" the threat and don't move or protect your piece. He gets the best result if you make the worst move. The theory of games is based on the opposite hypothesis: adoption of the strategy that will give you the best results if your opponent makes the best moves.

In a children's game like paper, stone, scissors, the strategy is easy enough to figure out. To play the game, you display a fist in the shape of either a piece of paper (hand extended), a stone (bunched fingers), or scissors (two fingers open like scissors), and paper beats stone, stone beats scissors, and scissors beats paper. You have three choices, and it is easy to see, on the mathematics of the thing (leaving out observation and psychology), that the best strategy is to choose paper, stone, or scissors an average of once in three times, making their selection random, because any other strategy will be detected by your opponent. And the same thing goes for him.

Poker is very much more complicated. Indeed, so complicated is it that Von Neumann and Morgenstern had to simplify the game radically to examine the technique of bluffing, and even then one would have to be a theoretical mathematician of a very high order to follow the analysis.

They make the game two-handed, with no change of cards, and limit the bets, or bids (their term), to one on each side, high or low.

The description of their model, though quaint, is accurate. The point, they say,

"is that a player with a strong hand is likely to make high bids— and numerous overbids (reraises)—since he has good reason to expect that he will win. Consequently a player who has made a high bid, or overbid, may be assumed by his opponent— a posteriori! [when seen]—to have a strong hand. This may provide the opponent with a motive for 'passing' [folding].

"However, since in the case of passing the hands are not compared [winners don't show], even a player with a weak hand may occasionally obtain a gain against a stronger opponent by creating the (false) impression of strength by a high bid or by an overbid—thus conceivably inducing his opponent to pass [i.e. bluffing].

The authors immediately note that whether this really is the motive for bluffing is open to doubt.

"Actually a second interpretation is conceivable. That is if a player is known to bid high [bet strongly] when his hand is strong, the opponent is likely to pass in such cases. The player will, therefore, not be able to collect on high bids, or on numerous overbids, in just those cases where his actual strength gives him the opportunity. Hence it is desirable for him to create uncertainty in the opponent's mind as to this correlation [mix it up]—i.e., to make it known that he does occasionally bid high on a weak hand."

Thus the essential conundrum of poker: Has he or hasn't he got what he says he's got?

"Of the two possible motives for bluffing," Von Neumann and Morgenstern sum up, "the first is to give a (false) impression of strength in (real) weakness; the second is the desire to give a (false) impression of weakness in (real) strength. Both are instances of inverted signaling, i.e., of misleading the opposition." The analysis shows that it is the second motive, the need to induce calls when you hold strong hands, that makes the bluffing pay off.

Very well; but how often do you bluff to make it pay off? The analysis given is far too complex for ordinary mortals (certainly this player) to follow, but what the results show is that "there exists one and only one good strategy in the form of Poker under consideration.

"On a sufficiently strong hand, the player should bid high and nothing else. On weaker hands, however, the player should bid irregularly high and low, more precisely to bid mostly low but with occasional irregularly distributed bluffs."

The first part of this recommendation, always to bet high on strong hands, is not to be taken as a general rule, of course. The practice of checking cinches, or very powerful hands, if not overdone, sometimes pays off handsomely as a way of getting the other man to bet his hand, to bet into yours. There is the risk that he will just check along for nothing, but if his hand is that poor, he wouldn't see a big bet from you anyway, would he? The point in this context is that Von Neumann's simplified game did not allow enough reraises to make this worthwhile.

Was so much higher mathematics necessary to reach this not so startling conclusion about the "good strategy"? The answer is that the study simply took poker as one practical exercise in a comprehensive investigation of game theory; it was not concerned with poker as such. The findings, all the same, give a scientific basis to the generally assumed rule drawn from experience: that successful play depends not simply on varying your betting by bluffs, but that it is essential to bluff weak hands, and sometimes be called, in order to make the high hands pay.

What is probably the crucial conclusion of the study is not at all obvious, though. It is the warning that any *deviation* from the "good strategy" leads to immediate losses. Incorrect bluffing, i.e., too frequent or infrequent bluffing, will make you lose against an opponent who is himself playing the good strategy. He could then cause you to lose even more by deviating from the strategy himself, but if you reverted to the good strategy he would then suffer, "i.e., the importance of bluffing lies not in the actual play, played against a good player, but in the protection it provides against the opponent's potential deviations from the good strategy." Correct bluffing protects you against too much or too little bluffing from the opposition.

The good strategy in this variant of poker is not permanently optimal, regardless of your opponent. Against a bad player, there are obviously other strategies you could adopt which would work even better. Just as in chess, against a good player you would not normally depart from the correct opening line in the first few moves, whereas playing against someone who knows nothing about chess openings, there are all sorts of traps you can set which he won't know about. The warning that "no permanently optimal strategy exists" simply means that you have to know your man.

Every poker player knows the basic odds, that in five-handed draw you need at least jacks to open, that at seven card stud the average winning hand is aces up, and so on. Those odds are merely a frame of reference. Bluff turns the laws of probability inside out. Assessment of a hand involves not just its strength as five cards, but its relative value measured against position, what's out against you, and the personalities of the other players involved. During the game, a player makes this kind of calculation, as it were, intuitively. He does not consider each item separately and then draw up a balance sheet; the whole operation is a reflex.

There are, in fact, two kinds of odds, card odds and investment odds. The card odds are the probabilities of being dealt or drawing to various hands. For instance, a pat full house is dealt once in seven hundred hands (which doesn't mean two won't be made in the same deal), and if you get one, you know it's good without the aid of statistics. By contrast, drawing to two pairs, which is a regular occurrence, coming up once in twenty hands, the odds to make a full house are "only" 11 to 1. Yet the pot seldom makes it worthwhile to draw in money terms. Most players play roughly according to the card odds, whereas what really count are the investment odds, what you will win if you hit. According to Amarillo Slim, who won the World Championship in 1972, "There are probably not even forty people in the United States who know the proper percentages involved in drawing out on a hand," which is a Texan's way of saying "It's not as easy as you think, buddy."

The best account in a poker book at defining the kind of thought process that most players develop, on the lines of "He's probably got such and such and I've got this, and if I draw a card and improve, and he doesn't hit, I should win a nice pot," is given by Frank Wallace in *The Advanced Concepts of Poker* (1968) as follows:

$$\frac{\text{potential size of pot x probability of winning pot}}{\text{potential loss}} = \text{investment odds}$$

That is, if a player estimates that a pot is worth potentially $100, and that his chances of winning it are about even, or .5, and it is going to cost him, say, $30 (his potential loss) to play the hand, then the investment odds are

$$\frac{100 \times .5}{30} = 1.66$$

When the investment odds are greater than 1.0, the play is favorable.

For example, three players at draw each buy one card. The

good player, the would-be millionaire winner in Wallace's account (see Chapter Ten), holds two pairs, tens and fours. What does he do? He reads the table and estimates the investment odds as follows.

Draw one card to his two pairs: The pot will be worth about $200; the chances of his hand winning are fairly small, say .2; and the cost of drawing and then seeing the unimproved two pairs through to the end will be $60.

$$\frac{200 \times .2}{60} = .66 = \text{fold}$$

Draw three cards to his pair of fours: The pot will be worth about $300, because he will raise if he hits, though the chances of this happening are remote, say .1; but the cost of drawing will be only $20 (nothing further if he misses).

$$\frac{300 \times .1}{20} = 1.5 = \text{play}$$

The key to this play is said to be the high frequency in the second example of ultimately *folding* because of the times he fails to hit the third four. The occasions when he has to call are so few (on that basis he might just as well draw on the tens, it seems to me) that the cost is relatively small. Maybe so. My own fear would be catching another four; it's still a very weak hand if anyone else starts raising, though the bluffing possibilities are considerable.

Could one insert into this kind of formula a factor to express the value of a bluff? Let's say you miss the third four and still bet the pot. Will they believe you? More precisely, will they believe you four times out of five? If so, in this example the bluffer wins $300 four times for the cost of one bluff. But if that loss comes up the first time, will they believe you the next time? Presumably, being seen changes the equation as a whole. You might then reckon it's 50-50 you'll be called next time. But that means when you really have a hand and bet it as if you were running the same bluff, you're more likely to get the calls you want. Bluff can never be pinned down so exactly.

What matters in bluff is instinct, above all a sixth sense of an opponent's weakness. You are not going to bluff a man when he has a lock, after all. But if something tells you he is not entirely confident—it could be a hesitant bet, a quaver in the voice, a sudden untypical gesture revealing strain under fire (Slim claims he can spot a nervous movement of a muscle in the throat), or any other half clue—then you go with your hand and bluff it. At that point all the mathematical calculations of odds and cards and money go out the window. Against tight players, a four flush bet aggressively could turn into a winning hand, whereas if an inveterate caller is in the pot, determined to keep you honest, no amount of money on the final bet will push him out. It's all according. Which is not to say that theoretical formulae don't have their value, only that man cannot win by math alone.

To go from the sublime to the Heath Robinson: How about wiring poker players to lie detectors to test their reactions while playing? This somewhat bizarre analysis of bluffing was actually conducted back in 1925 by a psychologist named Ethel M. Riddle. This lady hit on the idea of using lie detectors, i.e., breathing measurement equipment, to gauge players' aggressive instincts in the course of a session ("the game, although it consists largely of trained responses, allows for a spontaneous release of impulses that is rarely permitted in the serious concerns of real life.")

A photograph shows six clean-shaven, white-shirted young students from Columbia sitting earnestly around a table looking at their cards. Behind them, slightly less-serious-looking lady operators are standing at their machines, ready to transcribe the data. Each of the young men is wearing a stethograph, an instrument for recording respiratory movements, carefully taped around his chest.

This experiment formed Miss Riddle's Ph.D. thesis, entitled *Aggressive Behavior in a Small Social Group,* which I came across while leafing through the files of the Library of Congress. She chose poker for her model because the number of players is small, each player can be easily observed, and in the form chosen, five card stud, it is possible to determine the stimulus to each player, in his own hand and from his opponents', as each card falls or each bet is made.

It was, apparently, a serious game that was played, however artificial. The only factor that upset the players, Miss Riddle says, was delay between the hands. (That certainly rings true.) The stakes were a 5¢ ante and a 20¢ limit. In addition, Miss Riddle paid her subjects $1 an hour for their time. Her findings were based on sixty-two hands, played over five sessions, during which the participants recorded, at the same time as playing out the hands, each time they tried to bluff an opponent and each time they thought someone was trying to bluff them.

As the experiment turned out, it proved very largely an exercise in the statistics of bluffing, rather than an investigation into the players' physiological reactions, for in that respect, the findings were minimal. "Although the rate and depth of breathing were both found to consistently increase with the playing, the total increase in lung ventilation was found to correspond only moderately with the degree of desire [to win]." One wonders, certainly with the more sophisticated equipment available today, if it might have been better to wire the boys to monitor their heartbeats. One also wonders, over allowing for what 5¢ and 20¢ could buy in 1925, if the stakes were high enough to produce much in the way of reactions.

Most questionable of Miss Riddle's deductions, in her analysis of the game, is that bluffing about 6 percent of the time is the optimum. It would be something of a revelation if such a neat formulation as this were true. What she found was that a 6 percent ratio of bluffing, in this series of deals, "renders the opponents less capable of judging when the player is bluffing and when not," while bluffing more often than 6 percent of the time was apt to lead to more frequent detection.

The trouble with this is that "detection" is not the be-all and end-all of bluff. It is not evident that Miss Riddle appreciated the value of bluffing and being caught once in a while for "advertising" purposes (as Von Neumann saw), nor, more importantly, that in a good standard game some bluffs may be in reverse, designed to persuade opponents that the hand you hold is *weak*, in order to get a call; in such cases being "detected" is the whole point.

According to the figures given, it would appear that the player who bluffed most often was the most successful at it. He was detected seven times out of thirty-one, which means he got away with it successfully twenty-four times; in addition to that, he was suspected of bluffing twelve times when he wasn't, which implies that he was quite often called or raised by the others when in fact he held good hands.

However, Miss Riddle seems more convincing in her general conclusions, put forward only as suggestions rather than established facts. First, a player's own word about the frequency of his bluffing did not really correspond with the amount of bluffing he tried. It was more probably a record of the occasions when he wanted to bluff or when he thought he ought to bluff or resist others' bluffing. Next, all the players were poor judges of when they were being bluffed. The number of attempts at bluffing by the infrequent bluffer was overestimated, while those of the frequent bluffer were underestimated.

But the most interesting conclusion, of all the facts brought out in the study, was that the winning player, or the one who bet the highest in the game, was the one whom the others most frequently tried to bluff out, and not the player who would be, in fact, the easiest to bluff.

If one thinks about this, it seems to strike a chord. Isn't it the high bettor, the swashbuckler, the come-and-get-me player whom one most frequently tries to challenge at poker? And if so, why? Perhaps to bring him down, to show he's not going to have things all his own way; perhaps to assert oneself in the game. An international bridge player, who made a good living at the game, once explained to me why a down-to-earth country businessman liked so much to play against him at his London club, though the privilege cost the man several thousand a year. He wants to go home to his wife and say, "Oh, yes, I bid four spades, doubled, against young Johnny this afternoon—you know, the England player—and made it with an overtrick." What he doesn't mention is that, in the course of the afternoon, he lost more than three thousand points at £5 a hundred.

As for a player thinking he was being bluffed, it was by contrast the weakest in the group, the one least capable of defending himself, who thought most often that the others were trying to bluff him (though none of the participants in the experiment would seem to have been very good at the game).

All in all, one must conclude, with regret, that Miss Riddle's findings are a bit sketchy. But they do represent a totally original approach that, one day, some psychologist or statistician might elaborate on in a more thorough kind of investigation.

I shall now offer a personal conclusion, for which there is no justification whatever in the thesis. It is that Miss Riddle was rather fond of one of the players. Anyway, she got her Ph.D. and she abandoned her psychological experiments.

HI-LO[*]

It is in hi-lo that bluff achieves its fullest complexity, combining the concealment of five card draw with the open card calculation of stud. As each card falls around the table at hi-lo, so the opportunities for bluff revolve, changing from card to card and player to player. The question isn't just, "Has he got what he says he's got?" as in classical poker; it's "Which way is he going?" and then "Which way can I beat him?"

One reason why hi-lo is so popular is that you can play in many more hands than classical poker. With more players involved, the action is correspondingly higher and the ways out, if you are in trouble in the game, are so various that hi-lo offers continual chances to courageous players and continual hope to losers.

Certainly without a high degree of bluff, or let us say opportunist tactics in taking chances, it is hardly possible to win at hi-lo. You may sit around all night at five card stud waiting for an ace in the hole, you may with patience recoup the antes at draw; but at hi-lo you will be wiped out unless you get out there and *play*. Nor is it much use hanging around for the kind of starters that poker manuals recommend. They're sound, all right—pairs of aces, three flushes and straights, three in the low zone—but such a pattern is too predictable; everyone will know what you've got.

At five card stud hi-lo, with a twist at the end, which is a fast-and-furious game with innumerable opportunities for chicanery, you can get involved with almost any starters—well, not anything; it depends on the situation, of course. But here's an instance of a bluff being carried through with exemplary consistency.

---

[*] I have adopted the spelling "hi-lo" because it looks sharper than "high-low." But for the words "high" and "low" I use regular spelling.

Fat Sam, a useful, fairly solid player, not overly given to wild plays, decided to run one holding (9)-Q. He raised on the first card, continued raising at every interval until the fifth card, and gave everyone the indelible impression that he was paired on queens. Two others were left in the pot, evidently going for low, and as ill luck would have it, on the twist at the end, one of them paired sevens.

Fat Sam meanwhile had not improved his lone queen.

$$
\begin{array}{ll}
(9) & \text{Q 2 5 10} \\
(A) & \text{7 4 8 7}
\end{array}
$$

The third man in, with (4)-A-8-2-9, bet his cinch, and Fat Sam merely *called*, a very astute move, implying to the pair of sevens, "Come on in, baby, I've got you locked with my queens back to back, so I'm not raising you out of this pot." The sevens stacked as a result of Fat Sam's call, whereas a raise—which in a limit game would not be too expensive to call—might have set him thinking and given him a clue to back in for the high. All right, these things happen. The point, rather, is that according to theory, you would be out of your mind to come in on a (9)-Q.

Or suppose you are dealt (2)-2, which in high stud is normally a snare and a delusion. At hi-lo this is a terrific bluffing hand. You may look like a low all the way along betting it up with (2)-3-4-8 and it will take a brave man to go against you; but let's say the last card gives you a second pair of threes. The paired hands are not going to suspect you for high, unless you raise prematurely, and you will slay them. I.e., if the pair of sevens in the previous example had *raised back* at Fat Sam, even if he had two queens, where would he have been then?

The complexities are like a maze in which a dozen different turnings open up ahead of you. (The various ways of declaring are discussed in Chapter Eleven.) This is the challenge of hi-lo. Bluffing does not consist in suddenly wading in with a walloping raise; it's a matter of gauging chances that are continuously changing. In practice, with experience of the game and, even more important, knowledge of the opponents, the range of possibilities can be narrowed down. You acquire that indefinable feel for a hand that tells you which way it's moving and who is trying for what.

Over all, one might apply to hi-lo the military or strategic concept of flexible response. Playing hi-lo requires continual responsive action. Each card to each player, each bet on each round of a seven-card hand, changes the situation. Assuming seven players staying in to the end, which means five betting intervals on which each player can bet, call or raise, there are, in theory, more than one hundred decision points to be registered in a single hand. Many of these will be checks or routine calls, but each move completes the pattern. Supposing only three players see it through to the end, there will still be more than fifty decision points in the hand.

One of the keys to success, perhaps the controlling factor in this responsiveness, is knowing when to fold what looked, at an earlier stage, like a winning hand. An instance of this kind of evasive action in a potential winning hi-lo hand is given by Albert Morehead in *The Complete Guide to Winning Poker* (1967). On the sixth card, you find yourself with a 7-5 low made and an A-10 flush.

However, the player to your left, who is tight, has been calling with a king, which, knowing his style, you suspect may be trips; and he has now hit open treys. And next to him, another conservative player, showing 6-2-J, who called the previous high bet by you, has just hit the case three.

Nevertheless, with one card still to come, you already have a powerful hand, which might well win both ways. Do you raise?

A	(A ♦ 5 ♦)	4 ♣ 3 ♦ 7 ♦ 10 ♦
B	(? ?)	K ♥ 7 ♠ 3 ♣ 3 ♥
C	(? ?)	6 ♥ 2 ♣ J ♣ 3 ♠

The answer given is: fold! The reason is that after B checks, C bets out. If you call, and B has his full house, he is going to reraise; and C—who probably has a six made (all the sevens have gone and a tight player would hardly have stuck around this far with an eight)—will reraise. It's going to cost you all your chips to find out. In this particular case, you would have to pay 80 for the chance of drawing the perfect deuce (in this game the wheel, A-2-3-4-5, works) to win half the present pot of 93, plus a half of C's losing call of 80.

Personally, if B bets 80, as a tight player very likely would when sitting on a full house, and C just calls, I might even reraise. Depends on how I felt. I would, perhaps wrongly, certainly come along for the ride for 80 chips because of the value if I do hit.

One can't really make these judgments away from the table. So much depends on your "feel" of the hand. What is perhaps a valid point to make about this example is that if A had raised on the first three cards, as he would be fully entitled to do with (A ♦ 5 ♦) 4 ♣, it would probably have forced a couple of other players out on the next round, and he would have held the initiative. On the cards dealt, this would have led to a different showdown, in which his low would have busted C, who lands up with a ten. This is not to "prove" the wisdom of raising early on a powerful hand, or to "disprove" the wisdom of folding when you are morally certain you're beaten. But it does illustrate the way that a single bet, like a shift in a kaleidoscope, can change the sequence of a hand. In other words, in terms of odds and chances, such a hand could be elaborated in any number of ways. There is no one answer because there is more to bluff than card values.

What's been going on outside the framework of this particular deal? Let's suppose that in the earlier part of the night Luckless Larry has been topped three times in a row by higher hands when he thought he was best. Is he going to bang his head against the wall now, a fourth time?

As it happens, poor old Larry has been having a spot of trouble with his business lately, what with inflation and strikes, and he is up to his neck in debt; quite apart from that, he isn't living with his wife and has a rather expensive girl friend on his hands, too. How does all that fit into the equation? Will it make him, out of sheer desperation, call any bet, however illogical?

Taking advantage of Larry's personal misfortunes? Perish the thought! All that side of his life is beyond the purlieu of the poker table.

Let's take an alternative hypothesis. As it happens, Lucky Larry has just been bought out by a conglomerate at a very fancy price. Money seems to have lost all value for him. What's more, last week his son was made captain of the school football team, and his daughter, who adores him, of course, has just won a scholarship. Good old Larry is feeling on extraordinarily good terms with the world. Will he call your bet regardless, out of a sense of self-indulgence when everything is going so right? Or will he be inclined to treat his good luck with respect and fold a potential winning hand in order to avoid unnecessary risks?

The judgment you make is not exactly the result of a conscious thought process, but unconsciously the kind of person Larry is will have a decisive influence on your decision in any bluffing situation.

To me, one of the attractions of hi-lo is that until the last card is dealt there's always a chance of staging some outrageous comeback. Here's an instance of how it can happen, even though the bluff was unintentional. It succeeded only because I was looking so damned miserable. The hand illustrates the kind of mistakes one makes when one is reading the hands all wrong, zigging when you should have been zagging, as they say at the Army and Navy Club.

It was the last round of the night, seven card hi-lo, declaration at the end by everyone coming up with a chip in his hand, and I had gotten drawn in, reluctantly, on a somewhat dubious low. It had started well (they always do when you're losing) but then I had caught a queen that hurt, and now on the sixth card I was trailing behind on an 8-6.

To my left, a man who bet only on sound values, the kind of player who when he gets ahead, as he was now, becomes ultracautious, was looking very aggressive. Showing three low cards to the six and three cards to an ace flush, he could easily be going both ways. I figured he had one or the other made already.

One other man was left in the pot, looking high, showing a medium pair. He was a strong bluffer, with plenty of nerve in tight situations, so when he checked the bet, I checked along; then when the hi-lo man, as expected, bet the size of the pot, the first player raised back 150. What do you do when you're caught in the middle?

$$(? \qquad ?) \; 7 \clubsuit \; 8 \spadesuit \; K \heartsuit \; 8 \diamondsuit$$
$$(6 \spadesuit \; A \diamondsuit) \; 5 \clubsuit \; 8 \heartsuit \; Q \spadesuit \; 3 \spadesuit$$
$$(? \qquad ?) \; A \heartsuit \; 5 \heartsuit \; 6 \diamondsuit \; 10 \heartsuit$$

Silly question. You fold, of course. The only thing was that the pair of eights' check and raise was obviously a brazen attempt to run me out, because it looked as if I was just hanging on to my low as a drowning man clings to the last life belt. Once I fold, his calculation is that with so much money in the pot, the first bettor will have to play safe rather than risk going against him with a flush, just in case his pair of eights is backed by a full house. It was not a very well judged bluff, it seemed to me, because if he really had his full it would be better to check it, to lure me into the pot. In any case there's no call for me in this situation against the possible six-low, but just because I saw through the high hand's ruse, I stuck it in out of desperation. First bad play.

To my chagrin, the hi-lo man immediately reraised half the pot. That meant he definitely had my low beaten, never mind his flush. The first raiser got the message too. Seeing his bluff was not going to work, he threw his hand in, not tormenting himself with a second glance, and I was left to decide whether to call the final raise.

It's always a very tempting situation in hi-lo when a seven-handed game is reduced to two players fighting it out. The chances seem to be even, if you can divine which way your opponent is going, to sneak in for the other half of the pot, even holding absolutely nothing. Of course if your opponent looks like declaring both ways, the equation doesn't work. But the really tempting part of this proposition was that I needed only one card for an almost unbeatable six-low. I reasoned, somewhat illogically, considering my previous bad play that night, that *he* knew I wasn't such an idiot as to chase him right through to the end without holding something pretty good.

So after a long hesitation (second bad play), I called. "Only" one card . . . There were maybe five or six cards to help me out, I estimated, out of about twenty left in the deck. On that basis, the odds were way out of line. And, of course, he too could improve on the last down card. But let's not count that chance. It was a case of in for a penny, in for the lot.

Without even looking at my final card (third bad play), I called for the remaining chips on the table. My hole card was a deuce, but it was still possible he would pip me with a better low. Indeed, I must have looked so riven at my bad play (no double bluff involved) that after reflecting a final moment, he decided to call both ways. He turned over a heart flush and 6-5-4-3-A. My 6-5-4-2-A was good.

On all the evidence and the odds, he made what seemed to be the right declaration and lost. (If you go hi-lo, you have to win both or lose the lot.) My bad play got me out of trouble for the night, and then some. It's not to be recommended, but only at hi-lo can this sort of high-wire act save you.

CHAPTER TWO

Origins

A man who can play delightfully on a guitar and keep a knife in his boot would make an excellent poker player.

—W. J. FLORENCE
Handbook on Poker (1891)

Gambling is one of the oldest of human instincts; poker is a fairly recent development. Poker *appears* to be about gambling, but it isn't. That's an important distinction that should be made clear at the start.

Let the losers gamble. The winners do not really gamble at all in the strict sense of the word—wagering money on a sporting event of uncertain outcome—because they know with a degree of confidence that amounts virtually to certainty that they will wind up winning, in the average run, regardless of the distribution of the cards. Their skills give them the winning edge. Of course one can be lucky or unlucky with the cards, missing a vital draw, or hitting a case ace. In the long haul, however, everyone gets the same cards, good, bad, and indifferent, just as at bridge, if you aggregate all the hands, you would find that each player gets an average of ten points. It's *how* you play them that counts.

The losers (bless their hearts) lose because they treat poker as a game of chance; they continually bet at unfavorable odds, not in the crude form of drawing a card to a flush when the pot offers less in money terms than the true value, but in the disparity of judgment, expertise, and mental concentration that losers show in relation to winners in the play of the cards. The winners win because, in this overall sense, they are always playing at favorable odds, and that is not gambling.

Why don't the losers do the same thing, if everyone gets the same cards? That is another question altogether, one that rests in the realm of psychology rather than cards (see Chapter Six).

The fact that the dividing line between poker and gambling is blurred is probably what has misled a number of English judges who have ruled on the issue. The authorities, naturally, have nearly always taken an adverse view of gambling.

In Henry VIII's reign, as in Greek and Roman times, gambling was banned because it interfered with the martial arts. The soldiery became so fond of cards and dice that they neglected archery. Accordingly, the state countered by making these games illegal if played in houses established for that purpose. (One could imagine in the latter part of the twentieth century that many governments would be only too glad to divert their citizens' energies away from shooting and into gambling.) The Act of Parliament of 1541, on which all subsequent English legislation was based, led to the distinction, on the one hand, between games of chance or chance and skill combined, and, on the other hand, games of skill alone; and this is what bedeviled the status of poker when it became an issue in the courts in modern times. Poker was ruled not a game of "mere skill" in the sense of the Act. (But is there any game that can *totally* exclude the element of chance?) It would have been gratifying to have persuaded the English Lord Chief Justice who in 1938 concluded that "it would be a perversion of words to say that it was in any case a game of mere skill" to have taken a seat at the table to try his "luck"; his Lordship would have lost his ermine and his wig in short order. After 1960, poker became legalized in clubs, which were allowed to make a seat or entrance charge, but not to "cut" the pot.

In the United States, where the individual states write their own gambling legislation, the position of poker remains something of an anomaly. According to the letter of the law, poker remains illegal in a majority of states; but so far as private games go, it is of course played everywhere.

Where commercial gaming is concerned, gambling should be legalized *for the gambler's sake*, to afford the people who need it the protection of the law. Typically, gamblers themselves receive least consideration. But as some expert witnesses told the Commission on the Review of National Policy toward Gambling (1975), it is desirable for those immediately concerned, and for society generally, that gambling activities should be conducted under the control of law, not as a special case, but on the same grounds that commerce or trade are regulated: to give the public a square deal. Poker ideally, however, is a private affair. And to those who object to winning money from friends, it may be said that it is preferable to losing money to friends.

Poker, according to all accounts, emerged in New Orleans, home of jazz and outlet of the mighty Mississippi, whose waters played such a major role in spreading the popularity of the game via the steamboats. Around the 1820's some French residents who had picked up a game called *as* in Persia introduced their own version to New Orleans. The Persian game, which goes back to the fourteenth-century *as nas*, was played with a pack of twenty cards—traditionally lions, kings, ladies, soldiers, and dancing girls—dealt out to four players. There was no draw. Hands were bet and shown, and the element of bluff was presumably what gave the game its excitement. In the New Orleans version, the values became aces, kings, queens, jacks, and tens. Straights and flushes did not count.

No one knows exactly how the name "poker" came into being. One theory is that the name was a Southern corruption of the French three-card game *poque*, possibly combined with the Persian *as.* It's easy enough to see how poque or poque-as could become pokuh or pokah. Another suggestion is that the name came from the German game *Pochspiel,* a derivation of brag, which involved a call by nonbidding players, "Ich poche." In any event, the game spread upriver via the steamboats and around 1837 was adapted to the pack of fifty-two cards, which meant that more than four players could play. The draw appears to have been introduced during the Civil War, when soldiers on both sides spread the game's popularity. Straights were ranked around 1860–65, flushes somewhat earlier. Stud and jackpots came in around 1870, to complete the evolution of the game in its classic form.

The first game ever reported, significantly enough, involved cheating. This is the celebrated account by an English touring actor, Joe Cowell (collected in *The Poker Game Complete*). He described a game he watched aboard a steamboat going from Louisville to New Orleans in December 1829 as "a high-gambling Western game, founded on brag, invented, as it is said, by Henry Clay when a youth; and if so, very humanely, for either to win or lose, you are much sooner relieved of all anxiety than by the older operation."

Cowell narrated what happened with great vivacity in his memoirs. It was a foggy night, the boat ran aground, and in the resulting melee, with everyone rushing out of the cabin to see what had happened, only the gentleman in green spectacles and a diamond stickpin (a sure sign!) remained at the table, quietly shuffling and cutting the poker pack, apparently for his own amusement. In all the confusion, however, he dealt out the hands to the wrong players and gave the hand he intended for himself to someone else.

"It was his turn to deal, and when he ended, he did not lift his cards, but sat watching quietly the countenances of the others. The man on his left had bet ten dollars; a young lawyer, son to the then Mayor of Pittsburgh, who little dreamed of what his boy was about, who had hardly recovered from his shock, bet ten more; at that time, fortunately for him, he was unconscious of the real value of his hand, and consequently did not betray by his manner, as greenhorns mostly do, his certainty of winning."

The next player bet the ten and raised five hundred.

" 'I must see that,' said Green Spectacles, who now took up his hand with 'I am sure to win,' trembling at his fingers' ends; for you couldn't see his eyes through his glasses; he paused a moment in disappointed astonishment, and sighed, 'I pass,' and threw his cards upon the table. The left-hand man bet 'that five hundred dollars and one thousand dollars better!'

"The young lawyer, who had had time to calculate the power of his hand—four kings with an ace—it could not be beat! but still he hesitated at the impossibility, as if he thought it could—looked at the money staked and then at his hand again, and, lingeringly, put his wallet on the table and called. The left-hand man had four queens, with an ace; and Washington, the four jacks and an ace.

" 'Did you ever see the like on't?' said he, good-humoredly, as he pushed the money towards the lawyer, who very agreeably astonished, pocketed his two thousand and twenty-three dollars clear!"

The hand that Green Spectacles threw away, which he had intended for the lawyer, was four tens with an ace. If the others had known a little bit more about poker, they might have asked him why he hadn't bet on it. It was the fourth-best possible hand he could hold, after all, yet he threw it away, without a bet. There is something rather engaging, all the same, about this rogue, with his flashy dress and his insouciance. Joe Cowell concludes his account with a prescient observation: "In that pursuit, as in all others, even among the players, some black-sheep and black-legs will creep in." His own memory is kept green by his colorful footnote to poker history.

At first, cardsharps were the boll weevils of these boats, but as the traffic on the Mississippi and Ohio rivers increased, so the reports say, some ships' officers saw a pecuniary advantage in having these gentlemen aboard, and became their accomplices. The gamblers were adept at every kind of cheating device—marked cards, reflectors, loaded dice, and so on—and found the wealthy slave owners and planters easy pickings. By the 1830's, it was estimated that there were as many as fifteen hundred professional gamblers working the steamboats between New Orleans and Louisville. The riverboat gambler, with his leather boots, his diamond glittering on his ruffled shirt front, and his long frock coat, has become the most elegant figure in American folklore.

When Robert Schenck was American Minister in London, he won the "very unjust title" of Poker Schenck. At one of the Queen's receptions he fell into conversation about cards with a noted English duchess, records W. J. Florence in his *Handbook on Poker* (1891).

"During this talk he described to her the beauties of poker in such a way that she became intensely interested, and begged him to write her out a set of rules and directions for playing the great American game. This Mr. Schenck very kindly did. The duchess learned to play poker, and as it wove its fascinating toils about her she wanted her friends to learn also. For convenience she had Mr. Schenck's letter printed in a neat pamphlet and distributed among her friends of the court circles."

Schenck's rules are a little terse. They begin with the deal and the somewhat questionable assertion that "the deal is of no special value, and anybody may begin." It is true that anybody may begin, but to be dealer, in the position of last to speak, has, of course, very considerable value at draw.

The extent to which poker caught on in America is reflected in the pulp literature that appeared toward the end of the century. In 1896 there was even a monthly magazine called *Poker Chips*, retailing little tales about poker. It survived only a few issues, but a number of stories and reminiscences that had some claim to merit were published in hardback, such as the collection *Poker Stories* edited by J. F. B. Lillard in 1896. Their engaging, would-be racy flavor is conveyed in this extract entitled "Mississippi River Stories."

"There's many a change up and down the Mississippi since I was a youngster," said an old man whom I met on the steamer between Memphis and Helena. "Before the war, sir, these boats were floating palaces, and the people who traveled on them were able to pay for anything on earth that could be supplied to them; and they expected the best of everything and they got it, too.

"The time to see life then was about the last of the year, when the planters were traveling home from New Orleans after selling their cotton crops. They would have, every man of them, a fortune in his pocket, and not one had the least conception of the value of money. As a matter of course there were gamblers on the boats. 'Where the carcass is, there will the eagles be gathered together,' the good book tells us, and it is true enough. There was always a game of cards—poker usually—going on in the saloon, and the gamblers seldom got the worst of it. I have seen many a thousand dollars change hands in a single game, for there was no such thing as a limit recognized excepting on the old law that a man had a show for his money. You couldn't make him bet more than he had. Men were very handy with knives and pistols, too, in those days, and more than once I have seen shots fired across the table.

"There was a mighty stiff game going on that night, and some pretty good players had dropped out one after another when the luck ran too heavily against them, but as fast as one man rose from the table another would take his place, and the game went on steadily till long after midnight. Two men sat all night, but luck was against one and toward the other from the first. The lucky man was watched closely by more than one in the room who knew him for a professional gambler, but although he must have known it he did not flinch. He played on as steady as a machine and took his winnings as calmly as though they were pennies instead of thousands of dollars.

"The other man was a youngster. He couldn't have been more than twenty-two or three, and although he tried to keep from showing his excitement he could not altogether hide it. He grew paler and paler as he kept losing, and those who watched his game saw that he got to playing recklessly and trying to force his luck.

"He lost over $8,000 before he came to the end of his money, but after a time he called for a show, putting a $500 bill on the table and saying, 'That's all I have.'

"I'll never forget the hands that were shown in that deal. Even the other players who lost took no pains to conceal their sympathy with the young fellow for his hard luck. One of them had a small straight, one had three aces and another had a flush. The youngster had four sevens and the lucky player showed down four eights. There was not the faintest show of emotion on his face as he raked in the largest pot of the evening—there was more than $3,000 in it—as coolly as he had done everything else, and picked up the cards, for it happened to be his deal.

"The young man was good grit. He did not say a word in

reply to three or four exclamations from the other players and the bystanders, but rose from his chair and turned to leave the table. Pale as he was before, he turned paler yet though, when he faced the man who stood before his chair. This was a stern-looking gentleman some fifty years old, but well preserved, and, as we afterward found out, with the muscles of a giant.

" 'Why, father,' exclaimed the younger man, 'I didn't know you were on board.'

" 'I got on at Natchez,' said the father briefly. 'How much have you lost?'

" 'All I had,' said the son in a low tone.

" 'And your sister's money?' said the father, speaking still lower.

" 'All gone, too,' faltered the unhappy young man, and he would have passed out of the saloon, but the father said very sternly, 'Don't go away, sir,' and took the vacant chair with a polite question to the other players as to whether he was welcome in the game. It was a form strictly observed, but objections were never made in those days to any gentleman joining in the game when there was an empty chair at the table.

"The son looked on with astonishment. 'Why, father,' he said, 'I thought you never played.' But his father paid no attention. His eyes were fixed on the lucky player opposite, and I, who was looking on very attentively, thought I could see a slight change in the latter's face.

"The game went on, but not in the old way. Whether I was right or not about the change of countenance, there was certainly a change in the gambler's play. He was far more cautious, and yet he began to lose. Once or twice he fumbled the cards as he had not done before, but I could detect no other signs of nervousness. One thing soon became evident—that the newcomer was playing at one adversary only. He betrayed no anxiety to win money from any of the others, but lost no chance to bet with the gambler. The others saw it, and one by

one dropped out, leaving the two to their duel. They all felt
that some kind of a story was being acted out, and were all un-
willing to interfere with it.

"After they were out the play grew higher, the father
forcing it at every opportunity. Twice he called for a fresh
pack of cards, and the gambler's face showed his annoyance
every time. The luck was against him, but that of itself was
not enough to make him nervous. More than one man in the
room had seen him play a heavier game than this with worse
luck and show no sign of emotion.

"Suddenly the climax came. With a motion so quick that my
eyes, at least, could not follow it, the elder man drew a pistol
and had it pointed at the other's face.

" 'Don't move a hair or I'll blow your brains out, Jim
Baisley,' he said, as coolly as he had asked for cards a moment before.

" 'I'm not moving,' said the gambler sullenly. 'You've got
the drop on me.'

" 'Yes, and I've caught you,' said the other. 'I told you
twenty years ago I'd kill you if I ever caught you cheating.'

" 'It's a lie,' said the gambler, angrily, but he did not move.
The pistol was at his face.

" 'A lie, is it?' said the other coolly, as before. In those days
to give a man the lie was to provoke a shot, and we expected
to hear the report, but none came. Instead the elder man
reached over with his left hand and suddenly snatched the
five cards the gambler had dealt to himself and which he held
in his hand. He threw them face up on the table. There were
three aces among them. Then, with another quick motion, he
spread the pack out, and three more aces were shown.

" 'You see, gentlemen,' he said to the bystanders without
moving his eyes from those opposite him. A chorus of curses
answered him, but nobody lifted a hand. We all felt that jus-

tice was about to be done, and a capable man had the matter in charge . . ."

The gambler drew a bowie knife and lunged at the father but after a short struggle he was thrown overboard into the Mississippi. Such is the well-deserved fate of sharpers in these kinds of stories.

A worse fate befell one of the very few (it seems) honest men who gambled out West, Wild Bill Hickok. As every poker player down the generations knows, his murder has been commemorated in the hand made up of a pair of aces and a pair of eights, known as "the dead man's hand." (Some say they were all black cards.)

In the winter of 1874, gold was found in the Black Hills of Dakota Territory and by the spring of 1876 Deadwood Gulch was on the map. Wild Bill, so the legend goes, looked down into the gulch when he rode into town and had a premonition that he would not leave alive. On August 2, 1876, he was playing poker in Nuttal and Mann's gambling saloon. He had not, on that occasion, taken a seat against the wall, which was clearly a basic precaution in those days when the Colt .45 was king. A nasty piece of work called Crooked Nose McCall, drunk and the worse for it, the story relates, sneaked in behind him and shot him in the back of the head. Another source has it that McCall had been hired as an assassin by a group of crooked gamblers who were afraid Hickok was going to be appointed marshal of Deadwood and would then clean up the town. Wild Bill slid to the floor without a sound, his fingers clutched tight around his cards, the aces and eights, with a queen (or some say a ten).

Wild Bill was a tough character who knew how to look after himself, as an earlier story of his life in Sioux City shows. Not the shrewdest of players himself, he had been regularly cleaned out by a sharp gambler named McDonald. Wild Bill's friends had an idea that McDonald wasn't winning on luck and skill alone and warned him to watch out. One night in a two-handed no-limit game, Wild Bill was drinking hard, and by midnight, though he seemed calm, he evidently became incensed at what McDonald was doing to him. He began to bet heavily on an apparently strong hand, McDonald raising every time. Finally came the showdown and McDonald announced three jacks.

"I have a full house, aces and sixes," said Wild Bill, throwing his cards face down on the table.

"Aces full on sixes wins," said McDonald. He turned up Bill's cards. "Hold on," he cried, "I see only two aces and one six!" Wild Bill whipped out a six-shooter with his right hand and replied, "Here's my other six." Then he flashed a bowie knife with his left hand. "And here's my one spot."

"That hand is good," said McDonald. "Take the pot." (Which reminds one of the player who suddenly plunged his bowie knife into the back of his opponent's hand, pinning his palm to the table: "My friend, if the queen of spades is not under your hand, I owe you an apology!")

Another famous story concerning a showdown at gunpoint is told of Bowen's saloon in Santa Fe in 1889. John Dougherty, "one of the Southwest's flashiest professionals," was playing a no-limit game with a cattle baron, Ike Jackson of Colorado City, Texas. Among the crowd of citizens around the table, for this game was the poker championship of the West, was the governor of New Mexico, L. Bradford Prince. Both men got big hands and $1,000 bills were piled high on the table. Running out of cash, Jackson wrote out a deed to his ranch and his ten thousand head of cattle. Dougherty, unable to call or raise, sent for pen and paper, wrote quickly and, handing the document to the governor, drew his revolver. "Sign this or

I'll kill you!" he shouted. The governor complied. Dougherty triumphantly tossed the paper into the pot. "I raise you the Territory of New Mexico! There's the deed!" Jackson swore and threw his hand in. "All right, take it," he answered, "but it's a damn good thing for you the governor of Texas isn't here!"

Even the Indians acquired a taste for poker. White-Geese-Sounding-on-Waters was a youth with such an extraordinary talent for the game that he was renamed Poker Jim. Some of the squaws showed a liking for it as well. In the Indian camps outside Virginia City, Paiute squaws who did the miners' washing in the early morning would pass the day playing poker till the men came back. George Devol recounts a game with an Indian chief in *Forty Years a Gambler on the Mississippi*, published in 1887, in which one of the braves kept wandering around the table muttering "Injun talk," but despite these signals, the chief still lost. Anyone who has a desire to play poker with "big Injuns" is advised "to play a square game and keep their eye skinned for the big buck that talks to the Chief."

Navajos used bad medicine on card players by stealing a hair from a man's head and uttering evil incantations over it. They also prayed to their gods to make imbeciles of their opponents at cards by removing their judgment and common sense, weakening their sight, arms, bodies, legs, and feet. This was called "singing downward" (and was no doubt a great alibi for paleface losers). Conversely, the Navajos sang upward, from feet to head, as good medicine to gain strength to win. In the light of the appalling record of the white settlers toward the Indians, it seems highly improbable that the braves' medicine was powerful enough to secure even an honest deal.

A bizarre account of how a Bannock Indian headman acquired, used, and then lost magical powers at poker is given in

Man in the Primitive World by E. A. Hoebel, the anthropologist. This story was told to him in the Snake River Desert of Idaho during field work in 1933.

"A long time ago [the chief, Running Water, told him] the Indians around here learned to play poker. I decided I wanted to be able to win at that game, so I went out to seek *poha* [power].

"I went out into the mountains to a place where I knew there were lots of pack rats. I wore only my breechcloth. I ate no food and drank no water.

"Continuously I prayed to the pack rats, 'Oh, pack rats! Here I stand, a poor, helpless human being. Take pity on me! Wherever you go, you gather everything in. That's the way I want to be among my people. I want to be able to gather everything in when I play poker.' For three days and nights I fasted and prayed.

"On the fourth night a big pack rat, the grandfather of all the pack rats, appeared before me. 'Human being,' he said, 'I have heard your prayers. I am taking pity on you. I shall give you my power.

"'Now this is what you must do. When morning comes, scrape up the scale that is formed by our urine on the rocks. Make a small buckskin bag to put it in and wear this always around your neck.'

"'Now I will teach you four songs. When you want to use my power wash yourself with dry wood ashes to remove all grease and paint [grease is held to counteract supernatural power]. Sing the four songs. Then when you go in to play poker, you will always win. You will be able to gather everything in, even as I do.'"

These things he did, and, according to his testimony, the power worked with great success until he got careless and cut in on a hand of poker right after doing a war dance—without washing off the paint in dry ashes. The effect nearly killed him and his power was destroyed forever.

One can only hope that Chief Running Water gathered in enough on his winning streak, when the magic was on him, to put him far enough ahead to withstand the bad luck that followed.

This approach, i.e., seeking power from pack rats, is based on two aspects of association: imitative magic, the assumption that like objects and actions have affinity for each other; and contagious magic, which assumes that things once intimately in contact retain an influence over each other—thus the talisman of the urine scale, or the casting of a spell over a hair from an opponent's head.

No need to feel superior to the Indians. What about your "lucky seat"? Or the ritual players so often perform in the way they get settled down, either in something they like to wear to a game or the way they stack their chips, compulsive little habits repeating a pattern of actions which is felt, somehow, to induce success. One man I know likes all the traffic lights to be green when he drives to a game, so he can get the feeling of everything going right for him.

Gamblers believe in luck; good players make their own luck by analyzing the chances and using them to their advantage.

What these stories from the earliest days of poker show is that the game was born with the three essential characteristics that have colored it through the years. It was a rough, tough game for the brave and the free; it was a game that rapidly separated the mugs from their money; and it was an activity that attracted cheaters. Over all, it had an air of excitement and danger about it, which still holds true. In the mining camps and shantytowns of the gold rush, when women were scarce and money was plenty, there probably wasn't much else to do but drink and gamble. There was a lot of poker and the action was fast and furious—that's what the movies say, anyway (see Chapter Seven). Poker itself exemplified the American virtues of independence and the will to win.

As the West was won, so the colorful characters of the gold rush were overtaken. Gambling was curbed or outlawed by the new states. It went underground or, where it was permitted, it became "organized." Big business, legal or illegal, moved in with its sordid syndicates and gangs. The gambling man, with his black Stetson and frock coat, his ruffled shirt and string tie, faded into legend as the last frontier was settled.

CHAPTER THREE

Presidential Poker

The commonest mistake in history is underestimating your opponent: happens at the poker table all the time.
— GENERAL DAVID SHOUP

What a pity Richard Nixon did not apply his poker principles to his conduct of the Presidency. From a personal point of view, he would have fared far better. And the Republic would have been spared much anguish.

Poker is a great revealer of character, a truism that applies to Presidents as well as to lesser men. The young Nixon, as it happens, was a good poker player, conservative but with a quick eye for the winning chance. What is surprising is not that he played well, but that as a convinced Quaker, he chose to play at all.

His first regular acquaintance with the game was in his early naval days in 1943, when he was posted out to the Pacific. Lieutenant Nixon, "Nick," as he was known then, though he may have had an idea of the game, was not a player; in fact, he spent his evenings in camp in such improving pursuits as reading his Bible. One night, however, he kibitzed the poker game in the Officers' Club and this evidently started a new train of thought.

One of his fellow officers, Jimmy Stewart, whom Nixon outranked as officer in charge of air transport at the base at Green Island by virtue of one month's seniority, has recalled in *The Real Nixon* by Bela Kornitzer (1960) how he taught Nixon to play.

"One day I noticed Nick lost in his thoughts. He was seemingly concentrating on some problem. Finally he asked: 'Is there any sure way to win at poker?' I explained that I didn't know of a sure way to win, but that I had a theory for playing draw poker. It was that one must never stay in unless he knows he has everyone at the table beaten at the time of the draw. Nick liked what I said. I gave him his first lessons. We played two-handed poker without money for four or five days, until he had learned the various plays. Soon his playing became tops. He never raised unless he was convinced he had the best hand."

In the next two months, Nixon won $6,000. Every successful player has to go through his initiation to the game. Once upon a time it was in the colorful setting of frontier saloons, more likely nowadays it begins in college; Eisenhower learned even younger, but he was too darned nice to win off his fellow officers.

Nixon was lucky, right at the start, to find a man prepared to ground him so carefully; but he deserved full marks for taking the trouble to learn in this way. He took the game very seriously, even if it was a "friendly" game, always tossing his winning hands in the discards and mixing them up if he won the pot unseen, so as to avoid giving his game away. Clearly, he learned not just what the "rules" or percentages are, but that sense of their limitations that teaches a good player when to ignore them and, if necessary, turn them inside out.

Another friend who served with him in the Pacific, James Udall, went so far as to declare that " 'Nick was as good a poker player as, if not better than, anyone we had ever seen. He played a quiet game, but wasn't afraid of taking chances. He wasn't afraid of running a bluff. Sometimes the stakes were pretty big, but Nick had daring and a flair for knowing what to do.' " Udall observed that, watching him closely, his fellow officers prophesied that he would succeed in whatever civilian career he might choose. That he would become President, however, did not, presumably, show in the cards.

Why did Nixon pass over the traditional Quaker objections to gambling? The explanation given is that he needed the money. He improved his poker to such an extent that he won "a sizable amount." How much money there was in those games we don't know. But he did tell Stewart that poker laid the foundations of his political career, because his winnings enabled him to finance his campaign against Congressman Jerry Voorhis.

Later on, from the eminence of the Vice-Presidency, Nixon deprecated his talent for poker. Dr. Albert Upton, his former drama coach at Whittier College, California, was convinced that a man who couldn't hold a hand in a first-class poker game was not fit to be President of the United States. Nixon's reply, when the question was put whether he agreed with this prescription, was rather too modest: " 'I believe my ability in this field is somewhat exaggerated,' he declared. 'I was fairly successful playing poker overseas. During the lull in the bombardments, when we didn't have anything else to do, men from the various neighboring islands would get together in the evenings for games, and it wasn't always poker.' "

He added that he had played only once since becoming Vice-President and on that occasion " 'just broke even.' " "Just breaking even" is the habitual language of a winner disguising for one reason or another his success. As a politician (indeed, like most winners), Nixon became extremely coy when pressed about figures.

A severe but judicious summing up comes from Garry Wills's *Nixon Agonistes* (1970):

"After the war he gave up poker entirely. It had served its purpose. The essential Nixon traits are all here. First, the justification. 'He needed the money.' To some men it would seem wrong to be playing for anything but amusement—or at least to be playing without amusement. But for Nixon, the 'self-improving' note is a moral necessity. And if you are going to do anything at all, you should make it useful; the devil's playground can become the saint's joyless field of exercise. It helps, watching Nixon's 'ruthless' singlemindedness when bigger pots have been at stake, to remember those poker days."

Or, to bring the scene more up to date, to his resignation as President in 1974, Nixon should have remembered the principles he used to uphold: never to stay in the pot unless he had everyone beaten before the draw, never to raise unless convinced he had the best hand.

The Watergate cover-up turned into a poker game on a national scale. It was, in an obvious sense, the biggest bluff that Nixon ever ran, the basis of which was that if the full weight and prestige of the Presidency were committed to the cover-up, Congress would not "see."

The reason this strategy did not succeed was not that the bluff itself was entirely misconceived; after all, the White House had the immense advantage of running the game, so to speak, and of exercising its control over the principal players. The bluff failed in the end because *the hands were recorded* in the form of the tapes. That was why the cover-up was ultimately exposed. If the tapes had been destroyed instead of being doctored, the probability is that Congress would not have nerved itself to bring in a Bill of Impeachment, and Richard Nixon's greatest bluff would have "held"—"succeeded" is not quite the right word because the game by that time was out of the President's own control.

The President who really enjoyed his poker, and who went on playing during his term at the White House, was Harry Truman. He was the kind of bright and breezy player you would expect of the man who immortalized the expression "The buck stops here." (The buck is a counter that is passed around the table to designate the man who has to ante up and deal. Hence the phrase, "Passing the buck.")

Surprising as it may seem, the most portentous act of state of modern times took place against the background of a continuous poker session: the decision to drop the atomic bomb on Hiroshima. It took place just before the end of the war with Japan, after the Big Three meetings at Potsdam. Truman, in office less than four months, beset by fearful problems, was seeking a few days rest at sea aboard the cruiser *Augusta*.

Poker was the main activity aboard ship, according to Merriman Smith, then White House reporter for United Press, so much so that the Secretary of State, James Byrnes, felt obliged to tell Smith off. " 'Why in the world don't you leave the President alone?' the Secretary of State demanded. 'Give him time to do something besides play poker.' 'Leave *him* alone?' Smith protested. 'We don't start those games. He does.' " It seems that Truman deliberately kept the games going in order to avoid having to spend his time talking to Byrnes. The press was far more entertaining company, and it wasn't hard to see why.

The President played poker morning, noon, and night. The stakes were fairly high, pot limit, and frequently ran into hundreds of dollars. Poor Byrnes waited in the wings for a chance to resume his talks with Truman, but the President's only free time was early in the morning, before breakfast, or at mealtimes. The shipboard games started as early as 8:30 or 9 o'clock in the morning and, with brief stops for lunch and dinner, usually ended sometime toward midnight.

One morning a Marine orderly turned the reporters out of bed before 8 o'clock with a summons to report to the flag cabin in fifteen minutes. " 'Why don't we play all night instead of starting out at this awful hour?' " one of the reporters complained. But this was not a call to break open a deck of cards for a new game. Instead, the President reviewed in great detail the development of the atomic bomb and its forthcoming explosion over Hiroshima. "Once this graphic secret was told to us for later publication, out came the cards and chips."

This sidelight on such a momentous decision is revealing. It is not, it almost goes without saying, a shocking proof of Truman's acting callously or superficially in the face of great events. On the contrary, we know that the decision to use the atomic bomb was weighed, as it had to be, with infinite care, and that the main motivation in employing it was to shorten the war and so save lives in the Pacific. We also know from his own account that Truman (unlike many of the scientists involved and some others directly concerned in the event) had no doubts. But he was, evidently enough, under great strain during those days, as who would not be, and he sought relief from this in playing poker with the press. Should we think any more of him had he played golf, like Eisenhower, to fill in time before a major decision of state, or withdrawn to the upper deck with an easel, as Churchill might have done? Poker has this advantage: it is a social activity which involved the President directly with congenial company.

Truman was not an all-out gambler. Poker was a kind of safety valve. Moreover, he had a basic streak of kindness in his play and became quite embarrassed when he won heavily playing against comparatively lowly paid reporters. On occasion his generosity led him to stay on utterly impossible hands, in an attempt to throw money back into the game; his luck, however, was so good that he sometimes hit inside straights while trying to give back his winnings, and so won even more. He was never seen to lose badly in those days.

As for his play itself, he did not hesitate to take calculated risks. He played a forthright, hard-hitting game and seemed to bluff mainly out of playful mischief or boredom resulting from a long run of mediocre cards. His game was based more on analysis of the other players than strictly on the cards themselves; precisely the opposite of Nixon's technique, it appears.

Truman cared little about the size of the stakes, as another incident recalled by Merriman Smith in his affectionate memoir shows. The game was in the basement recreation room of the house of one of Truman's old friends in Independence. The limit was 25¢, but the President was never seen to play more vigorously. He was delighted by the tightness of the game. One of the players was a gentleman in his eighties. He was so cautious that at five card stud he checked a pair of kings back to back. Smith, showing two sevens, bet the limit all the way, and on the last card drew a third seven, while his opponent drew a second king showing. Smith with three of a kind bet a quarter, the old-timer called and raised, and when Smith reraised, the old man merely called the bet, turning up his third king in the hole. Truman roared with laughter. "'You smart city fellers,' he hooted. 'You let the oldest man in Independence show you up for a beginner.'"

Of course Smith might have realized when the old man kept calling his sevens that he had to have kings wired. But still, at 25¢ raises, why should he be so careful?

Truman stood up and told them to keep the game going. "'I've got to get home. It's way after my bedtime.'"

The old-timer bobbed a good night to the President and looked at his watch. It was 10:45. "'Harry,' he observed dryly, 'must be about even.'"

Wars and soldiering in general, when time is on men's hands, always encourage gambling. March 1772 was a disastrous season for George Washington. Serving at Williamsburg, he lost £39.11.3 in twelve games and won only £17.17.6 in five.

The general's account books show that both before and dur-

ing the Revolutionary War, playing cards was one of his favored pastimes. He recorded meticulously every penny he
spent or received, and played regularly. He is said to have
played "post and pair," a bluff game with some similarity to
poker, and often won or lost several pounds a night, big
money in those days.

He kept a page in one of his ledgers headed "Cards and
Other Play," listing his games at Mount Vernon (home) and
nearby towns (away), as a football team does. The record at
the end of the ledger suggests that Washington's skill at the
card table was only middling.

> 1775   January 1 . . . . By Bal[ance] against Play
>   From Jan, 1772 to this
>   date . . . . £6   3s.   3d.

So he came out on the plus side—just.

Since the general's record shows he won fewer times than
he lost, he evidently kept his losing nights within bounds. It
may be that junior officers who make a practice of whipping
the commander in chief at cards don't go far in the army, one
commentary on Washington's diaries suggests, adding: "So it
is not likely that the general had to put his losings on the expense account during the war, as modern writers sometimes
do under 'entertainment.'" One or two reporters in Truman's
entourage had to pad their expenses for weeks to get their
losings back.

Another soldier-President who found winning hard to take
was Ike. He had learned the game as a boy and learned it
well, from an old hunter and woodsman, Bob Davis, out in the
wilds of Kansas.

"He dinned percentages into my head night after night
around a campfire, using for the lessons a greasy pack of
nicked cards that must have been a dozen years old. We

played for matches and whenever my box of matches was exhausted, I'd have to roll in my blankets and go to sleep."

Bob used to take him on hunting and fishing trips, and although he could barely sign his own name, he certainly understood percentages at poker.

As a youngster, Ike was fascinated by the game, he says in his memoir *At Ease: Stories I Tell to Friends*. So thoroughly did Bob Davis drill him on percentages that he continued to play poker until he was thirty-eight or forty and was never able to play a game carelessly or wide open. "Since most tyros and many vets know nothing about probabilities, it was not remarkable that I should be a regular winner." In fact, Ike was too successful, for he adds: "When I found officers around me losing more than they could afford, I stopped playing."

As colonels, he and George Patton played twice a week in a game with some other officers. Normally they insisted on playing "with bachelors or others who could afford to lose. But there were a number of men going through the camp for discharge who had money to burn . . ." One such man who appeared every night, Ike recalls, was a "uniquely unskilled player" who made him think of the old maxim of Hafiz:

> "If he be young and unskillful
>   plays for shekels of silver and gold
> take his money my son praising Allah
> the fool was made to be sold."

However, Ike was shocked out of this attitude when the man came to him one morning and asked whether he would take government bonds to pay for his losses of the night before. It turned out that these were "Baby Bonds," saved by his wife in the years he had been away fighting. Ike accepted them, but later he "felt like a dog." After thinking it over, he talked to the others about it. They tried to remember how much the man had lost in the game, which was a considerable sum, and agreed to find some way of letting him get his money back.

"We didn't want to hurt his pride by making him a charity case, so we decided to allow him to win. In our belated compassion, we agreed that he ought to win back not only the Baby Bonds but something extra. This was not achieved easily. One of the hardest things known to man is to make a fellow win in poker who plays as if bent on losing every nickel. Our system was to guess when the man we were trying to help had a good hand. Then we'd step in to drive everybody out. After we had driven them out with betting, which wasn't easy to do without driving the principal out, we'd let him win the hand.

"It was trouble. For example, at one point the captain, my adjutant, found himself with a good hand. If he were called, he would have won easily. Since he had already drawn, it would have looked silly for him to throw in his hand. The only way to disqualify himself was to have too many cards. While the others were picking up their hands, he dropped his cards on one that was lying in front of him, and then said: 'I'm sorry. I called for two cards and wanted only one. Now I have six cards. My hand is dead.' That was just one stratagem. But it took until nearly midnight to get the job done. Finally the game broke up."

Ike then went to Colonel Patton, the man's commanding officer, and suggested that he issue "an order that no one in his brigade be allowed to play cards for money." The next day the man dropped in on Ike. " 'You know what's happened? Old Patton has just stopped card playing for everybody in his brigade. Isn't that just my luck—just as I was started on a real winning streak?' " (He must have been a *very* bad player.)

Ike decided he had to quit playing poker then. It wasn't because he "didn't enjoy the excitement of the game," he says; he really loved to play. But he felt it was no game to play in the Army. Ike's steady, precise play, sound if uninspired, fits with his general character: no risks. One would imagine rip-roaring stuff from George Patton.

Unless, like me, you've played there, it is hard to believe, looking down from the elegant heights of Capitol Hill, that Washington was a gambling town in its early days. "The Hall of the Bleeding Heart," the sobriquet given to Edward Pendleton's Palace of Fortune, opened in 1832, was a success from the start. In those faction-ridden days of the 1840's and 1850's, we are told, gaming houses were the only places where abolitionists and secessionists were seen together.

Ascending the steps of the Capitol one day, so the story goes, Thaddeus Stevens, the radical Pennsylvania abolitionist, known as one of the best poker players in Washington, was approached by a black preacher seeking a contribution for his church. Stevens, who had cleaned up in a game the night before, turned out his pockets, observing reverently, "God moves in a mysterious way . . ."

Most gaming rooms were on or around Pennsylvania Avenue, a short ride from the Capitol, a tradition admirably carried forward in modern times by the cardroom of the National Press Club on 15th Street and Pennsylvania Avenue.

Of all nineteenth-century politicians, nobody better personified the swashbuckling, high-gambling poker player than Henry Clay. In the Presidential election of 1832, when he was thought to be the only man who might beat Jackson, his reputation as a poker player attracted some censure. One of his services to his constituents in Kentucky had been to soften the effect of antigaming legislation like the 1804 act to suppress gaming in the state. A hostile paper in New Hampshire claimed that Clay "spends his days at the gaming table and his nights in a brothel." He evidently enjoyed poker downtown quite as much as politics up on Capitol Hill. He once won $40,000 in a single evening in Lexington from a certain John Bradford. The next day Bradford confessed he couldn't raise the money. Clay did the gentlemanly (and the wise) thing: "Oh, give me your note for five hundred dollars and let the balance go."

Around Henry Clay have grown up some of the classic myths of poker, like his hand against Daniel Webster.

With Webster dealing, Clay drew one card on the draw and Webster stood pat. The two went on raising each other until each had $2,000 on the table. At this stage Clay stopped reraising and called. According to this account Webster laughed sheepishly and threw down his cards. " 'I only have a pair of deuces,' he said. Clay laughed too. 'The pot is yours,' he said. 'I only have an ace high.' "

Even if he thought Webster was bluffing, which he was, Clay had to put him better than just an ace. He would have done better to fold when his own bluff was reraised, and resisted the temptation to call the last raise. What is endearing about Clay is that he was a good loser as well as a good winner.

Then, of course, there is Henry Clay's theatrical dismissal of a member of the company whom he caught with an extra ace in his hand. "He slowly drew himself out of his seat, and rose upward until he seemed about seventeen feet all. He drew his pistol and the man made for the door. Clay did not follow him but expressed his indignation by walking around to his chair and shooting a hole through its center."

Bravo! Nor did Clay confine his high spirits to the gaming tables. He had an eye for a pretty girl, too. When John Quincy Adams accused Clay of offering a comely serving maid, "young, rosy and fair to look upon," a 5-franc piece for a kiss, Clay raised his accuser back with devastating effect. According to W. J. Florence's *Handbook on Poker*, Adams, who "seldom made a joke," had a weakness in his eyes that kept him constantly busy mopping up the tears. Clay was momentarily taken aback by Adams' charge, then pulled out his handkerchief and, wiping his eyes in imitation of Adams' gesture, told the assembled company that it was true. " 'I did offer the maiden five francs for a kiss, but as I attempted to take it she sprang from my embrace and indignantly exclaimed: "Do you think I am such a fool as to give you a kiss for five francs, when I've refused that old gentleman across the hall, who has offered me twenty with tears in his eyes?" ' "

Adams took the joke so badly he refused to speak to Clay thereafter. Eventually Clay apologized, explaining that he had been dumbfounded by Adams' remark, " 'the more so because it contained more truth than fancy.' "

In spite of the puritan spirit of the founding fathers, poker was not necessarily a handicap in public life, certainly not when it came to catching President Cleveland's eye.

" 'It chanced on a deal that I picked up a pat flush, Mr. Cleveland a pat full,' " as Henry Watterson, a Southern journalist and politician, recalls the story. Besides the President, the players included Secretary of the Navy Whitney, Senator Don Cameron of Pennsylvania, and Speaker of the House John Griffin Carlisle.

"The Pennsylvania senator and I went to the extreme, the President of course willing enough for us to play his hand for him. But the Speaker of the House persistently stayed with us and could not be driven out. When it came to a draw, Senator Cameron drew one card. Mr. Cleveland stood pat. But Mr. Carlisle drew four cards. At length, after much banter and betting, it reached a showdown and, mirabile dictu, the Speaker held four kings!

" 'Take the money,' exclaimed the President. 'If I am ever

President again you shall be Secretary of the Treasury. But don't make that four-card draw too often.' He was President again, and Mr. Carlisle was Secretary of the Treasury." (The odds to draw three more kings, assuming Carlisle could have divined that none were out before the draw, were about 650 to 1.)

The route to high office, no doubt, was not quite as direct as that ascribed to Carlisle, but it is pleasing to think that a Secretary of the Treasury might be preferred not for his close and cautious attitude to finance, but, on the contrary, because he had the inspiration and luck to make a long shot pay off.

Diplomacy has more in common with poker than does high finance. In general, one might say that the Russians play chess and the Americans play poker. The distinction is a broad one, but it's quite indicative of how the superpowers regard the world. At the level of grand strategy, the Russians are trying to change the world entirely, to recast it in their own mold. The United States, though ready to defend democracy as a form of government, is essentially aiming to meet each challenge as it arises, to win out.

Poker is ideally suited to the American temperament; it's fast, it's got action, it's a game in which daring and courage are the qualities that are most admired. Chess is slow, deep and reflective, and besides producing winners and losers, frequently results in draws.

When the Russians, with their mastery of chess, become involved in a poker challenge, they are at a disadvantage. In Cuba, Khrushchev was playing the wrong game, in the wrong place, for the wrong stakes. When the United States got drawn into Vietnam, it too was operating in the wrong dimension of a "no-win" situation.

President Kennedy did not play poker, so far as close friends like David Ormsby-Gore, British Ambassador in Washington

The Flow of Wisdom

at the time, can recall. But there was one episode—if such a cataclysmic chain of events as the Cuban missile crisis of October 1962 can be described as a mere episode—that did reveal certain qualities of judgment in the President which make one think he would have had a real talent for the game, and which vividly illustrates the parallel between poker and diplomacy. There is no comparison to be made, of course, between the missile crisis, where the "stakes," or the cost of failure, were thermonuclear war, and a mere game of cards; but the technique of negotiations, because it employed skills akin to poker, is instructive.

Khrushchev based his action, placing nuclear missile sites in Cuba, on a misreading of President Kennedy's character from the previous "game." At their summit meeting in Vienna, Khrushchev formed the conclusion that Kennedy was so young and inexperienced that he was not a man to be taken seriously. (Was it Mort Sahl who characterized the occasion by Kennedy's asking Khrushchev, "Can I have the keys to the car, Dad?")

Khrushchev's motives in constructing missile sites in Cuba may or may not have been justified politically by fraternal support for a small country threatened by a capitalist superpower; what is clear is that his confidence that he could deceive the Americans about his purpose, and then get away with it once they found out, was founded on his "winning" the Vienna summit in terms of prestige and authority. The effect of putting missile sites ninety miles off the coast of Florida was, like a sudden wild raise, to upset totally the nuclear balance of power. It was a misreading of the superpower game as well as a miscalculation of Kennedy's character.

According to Nixon in *Six Crises* (1962), "there is no doubt but that Khrushchev would have been a superb poker player. First, he is out to win. Second, like any good poker player, he plans ahead so that he can win the big pots. He likes to bluff, but he knows that if you bluff on small pots and fail consistently to produce the cards, you must expect your opponent to call your bluff on the big pots." Nixon was arguing that this was why "the two small islands of Quemoy and Matsu, and all the other peripheral areas," were so important "in the poker game of world politics." It seems a fair reading of Khrushchev's approach in October 1962 that he believed he had won the previous pots.

When the American U-2 reconnaissance planes spotted the missile sites, it was obvious to Kennedy that the United States could not tolerate such a transformation in the East-West balance. The new situation would put America in a position of severe disadvantage at the diplomatic level and threatened, quite literally, to wipe its cities out of existence. The question was: How to react? It would have been easy to "win," as Kennedy's chiefs of staff urged, by striking immediately at the missile sites. But the risk was that an act of such violence might trigger off retaliation, in Berlin or elsewhere, which would not merely put the Western alliance at risk but have incalculable consequences for the peace of the whole world—in short, blow up the game. If any other tactic could be found, the President (as a prudent player) wanted to safeguard the national interest in a way that would prevent the superpower balance from being shattered. The top brass couldn't see that the game as a whole was far more important than the hand itself, or, rather, that *how* the hand was won was what mattered.

As it happens, I have played in a few good games in Washington with one of the generals who had the wisdom to counsel a graduated response to the crisis, General David Shoup, Commandant of the Marine Corps at that time. Eventually, according to David Halberstam's history of the Vietnam entanglement, *The Best and the Brightest* (1972), Shoup became Kennedy's favorite general. Shoup was opposed to the invasion of Cuba, and would do a remarkable display with maps when the subject came up.

"First he took an overlay of Cuba and placed it over the map of the United States. To everybody's surprise, Cuba was not a small island along the lines of, say, Long Island at best. It was about 800 miles long and seemed to stretch from New York to Chicago. Then he took another overlay, with a red dot, and placed it over the map of Cuba. 'What's that?' someone asked him. 'That, gentlemen, represents the size of the island of Tarawa,' said Shoup, who had won a Medal of Honor there, 'and it took us three days and eighteen thousand Marines to take it.'"

From the outset, Shoup had no doubt that bombing the missile sites would be a great mistake. The way he put it to me (with no suggestion on my part of any parallel with poker) was revealing. "The Russians were bluffing. They didn't want a world war over Cuba. We had all the cards in our hand [in terms of missile capacity]; there was no way they could win. Of course you might say the U.S. was bluffing too, because we didn't want a world war either. But *we were bluffing with the best hand.*"*

* The general was a very hard man to beat at poker, as ready to sniff out weakness and call a $500 pot on a pair of sevens—"What can *he* have, goddammit!" he would demand—as to crack the whip on every raise when he stood best. "I haven't lost in thirty-two games!" he was wont to warn the company sternly, sitting down to play, a claim that was not perhaps absolutely watertight, but not so far off. Far the best thing about playing with the general, though, was that his authority was such that without saying anything, except occasionally snapping out the order *"Deal!"* he kept the game moving fast. There was never any comparing of hole cards after the hand, or dealing the next card off the deck to see what would have happened, when David Shoup was at the table. My own favorite memory of the general was his instant answer to my naïve inquiry as to how he would solve the Middle East crisis. "Draw a great big circle in chalk around the whole area, throw 'em all in the middle, and let 'em fight it out! Now, deal!"

Kennedy's immediate need, therefore, was to devise a response that would allow Khrushchev to back off honorably, to fold his hand with dignity. It was not a matter of Kennedy's "winning" but of Khrushchev's not "losing." Hence the idea of the blockade, or a quarantine, favored by Robert McNamara, Secretary of Defense, and George Ball, Under Secretary of State, to prevent Russian ships from ferrying nuclear warheads or other material to Cuba.

In this opening phase of the crisis, Kennedy needed time to evaluate the situation in case the photographic evidence of missile sites was somehow mistaken or in case Khrushchev was bluffing, and time to prepare the American response. It was a brave and imaginative stroke—a bluff of the highest order—when the President decided to continue to fulfill his routine engagements, including speaking on election platforms in various American cities. Likewise, the press was kept in the dark about the crisis. Panic was avoided; time was gained.

Kennedy also showed excellent judgment in strengthening his hand at home and abroad. In his own circle of aides, his brother Bobby, the Attorney General, labored night and day to get a consensus among the President's advisers, who were divided, so that the policy of blockade could be adopted with everyone in authority morally committed to it, everyone playing the same game. And in the United Nations, the Americans strove hard, and successfully, to enlist the support of the Latin-American group, thus giving the blockade at least the form if not the substance of legality in international terms.

The American hand was strengthened still further when Adlai Stevenson, Ambassador at the U.N., finally produced the photographs of the missile sites. This card was held back and played at just the right moment to have maximum impact in convincing American allies, and world opinion as a whole, that the threat was genuine, for Russian insistence that only

defensive weapons were being deployed in Cuba had under-
mined international confidence in America's protests.

What then of Khrushchev's reaction? The evidence suggests
that at first he believed America would "fold" and that his
original challenge would not be met. When the U.S. announced its blockade, twenty-five Russian merchant vessels
en route to Cuba were ordered to continue, and Khrushchev
deliberately raised the bet by detailing a group of nuclear sub-
marines to escort the convoy. Kennedy had matched this with
a raise of his own: aerial surveillance of Cuba was increased,
the Navy and combat forces were placed on full alert, and
these decisions were made known to the Russians so that
Khrushchev could see that, this time, Kennedy was not
bluffing.

By October 26, the eleventh day of the crisis, Russian vessels were approaching the American cordon, which extended
a distance of five hundred miles from Cuba. The blockade line
was far enough out for Washington to choose the time and
the place for executing this maneuver—like venturing a risky
bet in the final round of a big hand. In particular, Kennedy
wanted to evade, if he possibly could, a physical confrontation
by American Marines firing on or boarding a Russian vessel.
This would have provoked the showdown. The first ship to
be inspected on the high seas was very carefully chosen, a
freighter of neutral registry sailing under Soviet charter, not a
Russian merchantman.

Khrushchev realized, at this late stage, that Kennedy meant
to see it through. In the old cliché, the chips were down. What
had started out on Khrushchev's part as an opportunist move
against the U.S. had gotten out of hand. The stakes were now
far too high; there was a world to lose and precious little to
gain.

At the last moment, before the two sides physically clashed, with the risk of retaliation escalating out of control, the Russian ships were ordered to change course or turn back.

Some time earlier, indeed, Khrushchev had begun, without the knowledge of the Politburo, to try to sound out Kennedy, to play a hand within a hand, as it were. (The diplomatic record is narrated with graphic intensity in *The Missiles of October* by Elie Abel, 1966.) A Russian diplomat at the Washington Embassy, Alexander Fomin, presumed to be head of Soviet intelligence in the U.S., contacted John Scali, diplomatic correspondent of the American Broadcasting Company, and passed the urgent secret message that a deal was on: withdrawal of Russian missiles in return for an American guarantee not to invade Cuba. Kennedy (though not knowing whether the offer was genuine) was quick to respond, through Stevenson at the U.N.; the proposal gave the U.S. all it wanted and allowed the Soviet Union an honorable way out.

It was then that the Russians, seeking to extract the maximum advantage from the game in its new form, tried to up the ante with a further demand: that America should withdraw its Jupiter missiles from Turkey and Italy. The U.S. turned this down flat. Again, Kennedy showed clear judgment of what the game was about. The Russian missiles had to be removed from Cuba first, with no ifs, ands, or buts. Later, as the Americans intimated, they might reconsider their own missile installations, but that was a different and separate matter. (Kennedy had been trying for some time to have the Jupiter missiles removed from Turkey, but had been continually frustrated by the service chiefs' delaying tactics.)

What had happened was that the Politburo, informed of Khrushchev's private negotiations, the hand within a hand, was insisting on sending a much tougher message to Kennedy than Khrushchev's letter proposing a deal à la Fomin-Scali. When this second message arrived in Washington, it seemed to contradict the previous offer by Khrushchev. Kennedy and his advisers were confused. The stakes were being raised again, seemingly recklessly. They resolved the dilemma of conflicting signals by what proved to be a master stroke. They ignored the later message, which demanded higher terms, and replied to the earlier letter, which offered a practical solution. This again allowed the Russians to react in a rational way, to call off the ships and remove the missiles, to fold their hand without being humiliated if they chose to do so.

Kennedy's final move in the game was also in character: there was to be no impression given out that America had "won." The game was too big for national victories. As Khrushchev was to say (though his mistaken gamble prepared the way for his own downfall), humanity won.

CHAPTER FOUR

Puggy: World Champion

If you ain't a tiger, baby, forget it!
—JIMMY THE GREEK

High noon in the town without clocks. The sun reduces the screaming neon of the downtown casinos to a weak flicker, blanches the high-rise hotels along the Strip, burns out the empty lots. Only the desert throws back the light, unflinching. It's too hot even to cross the road.

The day revs up slowly. A few people are half-heartedly pulling at slot machines; a blackjack dealer flips the cards over as if in slow-motion; the craps tables stand empty.

Over in suburban Vegas, where the managers live in long, white ranch houses, noon is the waking hour. Sprinklers stand guard over the coarse grass, forcing the desert back. The patio doors are open, and the clink of ice chimes the hour; beyond the straggling line of roses the desert glowers and waits.

This is the morning after the world poker championship, and Mr. Pearson has just surfaced after three nights of continuous play.

Mr. Pearson is feeling ex-cep-tion-al-ly good. In his jacket is the comforting wedge of a huge wad of $100 bills, thirteen hundred of them, to be precise, bulging under his shoulder; and on the table, the Las Vegas *Review-Journal* blazons his name across the front page: WORLD CHAMPION. He has won big money before, of course. He has won many, many times in many, many games. And remembering his threadbare boyhood in a family of nine children in the Depression in Tennessee, the money is still important; but today the title means more than the money.

"Puggy" Pearson

Puggy (christened Walter Clyde) is a man in his mid-forties, bald, chubby, bronzed, a long cigar clamped into his jaw like a missile. Sure he feels good.

In the final hand of the championship, he has just scooped up $130,000 holding a single ace high. That hand was no fluke; it would have been worthy of a chess master.

Puggy seizes a deck and ripples off the top cards to lay out a poker hand on a coffee table at his side. The confidence he radiates—his ruddy, open, round face with his pug nose, his searing voice analyzing each card, calling the chances as they fall—is a total confidence, more impressive testimony to success than the house, the camper in the drive, the jumble of luxuries strewn around. If there can be such a person as a world champion poker player, Puggy sounds the part.

World champion? Can that mean anything at poker? Yes, in Las Vegas it can. "Even if I had'na won that hand," Puggy declared, in his rasping Tennessee drawl, a voice like a buzz saw, which cuts through the smoke and the betting and the kibitzers' chatter, "I would *still*'ve been the best player!"

The idea of a world poker championship was developed by Jimmy the Greek. In Vegas, naturally, the idea had to have an angle. The angle on this one was to create a new source of interest and publicity for the club running the show, which was Binion's Horseshoe in downtown Vegas, where the noise and the flickering lights and the workaday crowds and the merry clanking of silver dollars still give a faint echo of the good old frontier days.

Downtown Vegas has an earthier feel than the cool of the famous Strip, where the resort hotels loom over the vacant lots and where Jimmy the Greek has his office at the Flamingo. He staged the championship in the Horseshoe, rather than on the Strip, where it might have attracted a far bigger attendance, because of an old friendship with the owner; this setting gave the event a saloon intimacy.

Jimmy the Greek (born Synodinos on the island of Chios) is in his fifties, one of those soft-spoken, fleshy, powerful characters who own things and run things and who always have a piece of the action—even, in this case, a piece of Puggy in the form of a side stake in his winnings.

Poker, Jimmy claims, is America's national game, but it has no institutional framework, as big-league baseball or professional golf have. Games just happen, in every hometown. The best players do graduate, however—those who earn a living from card playing—and they move from game to game, always on the road, always seeking higher action. They gravitate, sooner or later, to Vegas, where the action can be found day in and day out, all the year round.

Some players go broke; others find their own level and stick to it; a few professionals reach a level of success where they are known and admired, like sportsmen or cabaret stars, accepted in the group of people who live off the gambling industry.

Jimmy the Greek, who likes poker but claims he doesn't gamble any more, saw that a championship would attract the top players and would be a plus for the club that staged it. The championship might, one day, be built up into a national event. In that case, there could be quite a few financial benefits—regular competitions, franchised playing cards and poker chips, who knows—if the angle was right.

In the championship of May 1973 the thirteen contenders in the final round were (with one exception) all professionals on the circuit, either playing cards as a way of life, like Amarillo Slim, who had beaten Puggy Pearson in the final the year before, or in the gambling business itself, like Johnny Moss, beaten finalist this year, who managed the poker at the Aladdin. They didn't have to be pros, but that was how it turned out. Quite apart from the standard of play itself, each contender needed $10,000 to sit down in the final session. That is a relatively small sum in the big games players like these are used to, but it was likely to be way beyond the spending money of most amateurs in town on a five-day budget trip to see the bright lights.

The preliminary rounds were less expensive to play in, and a number of hopefuls chanced their arm, including Jimmy the Greek himself. "I hadn't played in years. I was a little slow, but I wanted to see how I would match up." He was out-drawn, he complained, seven times in a row on seven card low. "I just like to play once in a while. Some people go out and have drinks and some people go out and have broads. I like to go challenge the best, to satisfy my own ego I still know what the hell I'm doing. I satisfied myself I was good enough to play if I wanted to."

What is the difference between a *good* player and a *great* player? Jimmy the Greek, with his soft voice, has no hesitation: "Concentration and the management of his money." He adds: "Being able to give up a weak hand, even if you tried to bluff it; knowing when to give it up as cheaply as possible. Sometimes you get stuck and you can't; you have to try and go all the way through. Puggy has that value. [Knocking hard on the edge of the table with a chip—*rat-tat-tat!*] He'll try to push the betting the first two times, maybe once and maybe twice, and all of a sudden he sees a trap set for him [*rat-tat-tat!*] and he'll check the last card."

Has Puggy got a weakness at poker? "His only weakness is he himself. He has no weakness playing cards. None whatsoever." Jimmy pauses for a long moment, thinking of hands gone by. "None whatsoever."

He speaks as if there were a mystical bond between the two, the attraction of opposites perhaps: on one side, he, Jimmy the Greek, a man who has lived in the big money a long time, who will lay high bets with the kind of men who like to make high bets, a manager of other people's gambling; on the other side, Puggy, open-faced, uneducated, still a country boy, but a *player* who has made it purely on his own skill, in a way, an artist.

The Greek goes back over a crucial hand in the championship. Johnny Moss had tried to run a bluff, had not realized in time that he wasn't going to succeed, and had not knocked on the edge of the table with a chip—rat-tat-tat!

Puggy had caught him.

"That's when that tiger is there to grab you. He'll pick you up. He's got a fantastic feeling in cards. Puggy's looks fool you, that pug nose and round face, that unbrilliant look of any sort. You just cannot conceive that a man like that is smart at anything. And he *isn't* smart at anything. Except one thing, and that's cards."

Hold 'em was the game played in the final rounds of the championship, a Texas game. Hold 'em is unlike any other kind of poker you have seen before, though all it is, basically, is a variation of seven card stud. Its characteristics are plenty of action, plenty of bluffing, and surprisingly low winning hands.

The game is played as follows: Each player receives two cards down in the hole, and there is a round of betting. Then three cards are dealt face up *in common*, after which there is another round of betting. Then a fourth card is dealt face up, followed by another betting interval, and lastly, a fifth card up, with the final bets.

The players can use any five cards out of the seven dealt, their own two in the hole with the five community cards, to make their hand.

"It's one of the toughest poker games in the world to play," according to Jimmy the Greek. "It's more like chess over checkers. It's all maneuvering. As each man goes around the table it's like moving your king, your queen, and your rook on the board."

It is no accident that this is a game played in the Southwest, and particularly in Texas. For some reason, most of the top-flight poker players come from these parts. Jimmy the Greek suggests this is because there wasn't so much to do, not so much entertainment, as in the rest of the country, so people learned poker. But it seems more likely that as poker spread westward with the Mississippi steamboats, it took more of a hold in the South and the West, and what with the gold rush and aura of adventure that imbued the West, poker became a part of the way of life. The best gin rummy players, by contrast, are to be found in New York City.

Are there any good poker players in Europe? Jimmy the Greek exhales slowly: "I haven't seen any yet."

The crucial hand of the championship, the hand when the flow changed, came like this: It's head to head, each player sitting either side of the house dealer, with the "railbirds," that is, the losers, the kibitzers, the passing spectators enjoying a vicarious gamble, crowding around the rail. At the start Moss had been winning. He hit two or three good hands and had an impressive pile of chips stacked up in front of him.

They were playing "freeze out," winner takes all of the $130,000 that the thirteen finalists (eleven of whom had now been frozen out) had put up at $10,000 each. Although Moss had about $85,000 in chips, to Puggy's $45,000, he did not look confident and his usually somewhat melancholy face was no brighter. Johnny Moss is regarded as one of the best three or four players in the country, but he was, at sixty-seven, probably feeling his age a little.

In this crucial hand, the decisive factor was position. Under the head-to-head rules, the player in the position of dealer antes $500 and the second man has to ante $1,000, making a pot of $1,500, with the dealer to speak first.

Puggy, dealing, was dealt the K ♥ and the 6 ♣ in the hole. He bet $500, a routine bet on a moderately promising hand, and waited to see what Moss would do.

Moss did not raise. He hit the table and said "Deal!"

"That means," said Puggy, going over the hand the morning after, "Moss ain't got nuthin'. No ace in the hole. He might have a little pair, but not a hand to raise on."

Yes, but couldn't Moss be sitting on a high hand, waiting to sandbag? Puggy rules it out. "How can you do that, anteing two thousand dollars? You've got to play! Johnny knows that. You can't just sit there and wait 'n' wait."

The dealer dealt the next three cards, the "flop," face up, Q ♥ K ♦ 3 ♠. Puggy then had (K ♥ 6 ♣) Q ♥ K ♦ 3 ♠, giving him two kings with a six, a useful hand but not too strong. Moss could easily be better. The question was: Did he have a king too?

Moss had to bet first after the deal. He checked, so he didn't have two kings . . . Puggy bet, Moss then raised him back . . . or did he? Puggy called him.

"I don't think he's got two kings! I don't think he can have king-queen in the hole. In his position he can't have king-queen in the hole and just call it at the start of the deal. He can, but it's not likely. He might have two treys and hope to catch a second pair.

"I just call it, in case he has got two kings. I can still hit a six and beat him. But if he's just got two kings and he ain't got sump'n with it, and I called his raise, he ain't going no further no way. He's going to stop and think—because what's two kings?"

The next card up was a 7 ♠, which makes two spades showing.

Moss pushed over a pile of chips, "a pretty good bet," as Puggy termed it, some $5,500.

Puggy thought about it and called. He sensed then that

Moss might be bluffing. He plays with him a lot. He knows Moss is, in fact, a rather conservative player. And Puggy has this feeling.

The last card dealt was 6 ♠, giving Puggy two pairs—a big hand—but showing three spades on the board.

Puggy   (K ♥ 6 ♣)
Moss   (?   ?)   Q ♥ K ♦ 3 ♠ 7 ♠ 6 ♠

Without any thought, no "analyzation," as Puggy describes it, Moss bet the better part of $30,000, all the chips Puggy had in front of him. A freeze-out bet, which would give Moss all the money and the title, and leave the loser with nothing but a very empty feeling.

Puggy, holding two pairs, kings and sixes, sitting foursquare to the table, looked along his cigar at the pile of chips bet against him, neatly stacked up by the dealer. The railbirds craned over, the chatter stopped, and there was a long, aching silence. Moss is a well-respected man in Vegas, but Puggy was something of a popular hero, even before this championship.

Easy enough to call it at $20 raises, or even perhaps for $200. But $30,000 is an awful lot of money. How long does it take a man to earn that kind of sum in his job? For most of us the time has to be measured over many months or years. Here it was at stake in the silent moment between one card and the next. Pug doesn't think of money while he's playing, though; it's just chips, a stack of chips.

Did Moss have his flush? That was Puggy's problem, facing his raise on the last card. He took a view of the hand earlier on, when the first three up cards were dealt. Then, when the last card hit, Moss bet quickly, almost instantly. Why?

"He cain't do that! I don't think he's got spades. 'Course he could've hit a fluke hand, somethin' like nine and four of spades in the hole. But I don't think he's got spades. That left me with kings and sixes. So I called him. He didn't have it. He had a nine and three of diamonds."

Not much of a hand to start with. But the point was that head to head, after having to put up an ante of $1,000, Moss was already *in* the pot. When Puggy opened the original $500, and Moss said "Deal!," he was already committed. He couldn't throw his hand away, and he went on to bluff it. And that's when the tiger was on to him.

As Moss observed dryly the next night, when he was back at his stand in the Aladdin, fixing up seats at the poker table for $5 an hour, it is mighty hard to call very big bets. The biggest hand he ever played was against one of the famous old-time gamblers, Nick the Greek, at five card stud. Moss, with a pair of nines concealed, had succeeded in luring Nick into a gigantic pot showing nothing better than an eight . . . and on the last card Nick the Greek paid to outdraw and hit a jack in the hole. The swing on that hand was half a million. Johnny Moss gives his wan smile and turns his head to hear a customer, dressed in typical Vegas garb of sunset shirt and trousers, over the typical Vegas background noise of slot machines. The man wants to know how hold 'em is played. "It's mighty hard to call that kind of bet, but he did it. Yes, sir! Now here's how hold 'em goes, it's a straightforward game, you get two cards in the hole to start . . ."

It might be argued that in the crucial hand in this championship, Moss played rather badly and Puggy was merely lucky. Would Puggy have called the $30,000 final bet if he had not hit the second six to make kings up? That would have been a harder decision, certainly; but on the evidence of the play, Puggy would still have seen it. He had seen high bets with lower cards.

Here is how he dispatched Jack "Treetops" Strauss (the nickname comes from his height), another Vegas veteran, who is in the same bracket of expertise as Pug and Moss. On this hand, Puggy "psyched" him out with a little verbal byplay.

Puggy was dealt 9-9 in the hole. The board came out 8-8-J, which meant possibilities of a big hand. Strauss at once took the lead in the betting.

Now, why would he do that? Puggy mused. "If you've got a big hand, are you gonna take the play away from me? If you've got an ace and an eight in the hole, are you gonna take the play away from me? Forget about it! You're just gonna call. What's he taking the play away from me for?

"Now, the next bet he made against me [fourth up card] was a huge bet! If he has got a big hand, what's he betting so much for? Then the last bet he made [fifth up card] was fourteen thousand! I mean, what's he got?"

The last two cards were both low, and Puggy, sitting on his two nines, did not improve. He had (9-9)-8-8-J-x-x, with a series of powerful bets against him. Did Strauss really have an eight in the hole, or a jack?

Here, in feeling Strauss out, Puggy showed another aspect of his card sense. He paused, made a move with his chips as if to put them in the pot, then pulled them out again, and said something to Strauss—probably something like "You got sump'n down there, have you, Jack?"—the whole episode being a stratagem to get Strauss to react, to reveal his strength.

Jimmy the Greek, acting as referee of the contest, thought afterward that Puggy went a shade too far in "coffeehousing." "That was the only wrong thing Puggy did the whole night. I told him so, quietly. It's one thing putting your money in front of you, as if you're gonna put it in; it's another thing to put it in and take it out.

"Sure, you can say anything you want in the middle of the hand. If Puggy had done that to me," Jimmy continued, "I would have said 'Flush!' or 'Two aces!' Now what's he gonna do? . . . Now you make him think about it. . . . You declare a hand that's a winner, the highest hand possible on the board. Is he gonna put the chips back in again?"

In fact, Strauss did not say anything, or anything audible. "He didn't give away his hand. Or maybe he did, to Puggy. Maybe that was what he was waiting for. Maybe he saw something no one else did," the Greek adds sibilantly.

What *did* Puggy get out of Strauss by this maneuver? "Well, it's not what I got him to say. Without directly lookin' at him, I made a move with my checks, and I said somethin' to him, too, see. I was kind of feeling there, you understand. And when he opened his mouth . . . I mean . . . I just felt . . . You see what I mean?"

If Strauss had kept absolutely mum, he might have had a better chance. But Puggy did not think Strauss was going to win that pot, no matter how he played it. "I wouldn't have put all that money in that pot to catch a third nine! Forget it! I thought I had the best hand. He was going to have to draw out on me when I've got two nines!"

So Puggy called the $14,000. Strauss had nothing more. The hand cost him about $28,000, and marked his exit. "He's a very aggressive player, and once he's knocked out of kilt, that's his downfall!" (At one stage Strauss played with an open umbrella behind him, so the spectators couldn't see his hole cards.)

Afterward Strauss went up to Puggy and said something that made Puggy chuckle, with his raucous Tennessee laugh. "He said to me, 'A year or so ago you couldn't play hold 'em. You could not play *at all!* You have become the only player in the world that plays my system. And I believe you play it better than I do!' " Puggy gives another great cackle. "He sure buttered me up!" The point being that there would be plenty of hands dealt in future games in which their rivalry would be tested.

By way of contrast, here's how Puggy played the best hand he received all that night, A-A in the hole.

The board came A ♠ 9 ♥ Q ♠. Pug wants everyone in the pot before he bets. If the first or the second or the third man opens it, he will just call, hoping someone hits a hand. Sitting last is a player named Bryan "Sailor" Roberts (he learned to play in the Navy), a genial, roly-poly Texan. He weighs in with a big bet. It's pretty obvious what he's got—two spades in the hole, more precisely the K ♠ and the 4 ♠. He reckons that if anyone else is going for the flush, he's got the "nut" flush, the unbeatable hand, with his K ♠. This is exactly what Pug wants, for Sailor to bet into him after the others are there. When it comes back around to him, Puggy puts all his money in the pot.

Sailor calls. He has eight cards to hit his flush (not the 9 ♠, which gives Pug a full house), and he hits it straight away because a low spade turns up on the next card. The dealer burns one and turns one and off comes yet another spade on the last up card. But this one is the 9 ♠.

When Sailor caught two spades, the dealer stacked up the chips and began to push them across the table to him.

"What are you doin', Sailor?" cried Pug, his voice rising. "I got a full house! Gimme that pot!"

"Hell, I didn't even see you had a full house," said Sailor ruefully. Sailor did not misplay the hand, Pug thought later. He was just unlucky to run into a big hand. All the same, when Pug put all his chips in the pot, Sailor was worst hand, by a long way. The point is that three aces don't need to improve; they're winning already. And even if Sailor hits his flush, as he did, there is an "out" on the last card for Pug, nine cards to make a full house plus an ace for four of a kind. Exit Sailor.

Not that threes of a kind are necessarily a sure thing at hold 'em. In a similar hand, with Q-Q in the hole and 6-10-8 on the board, Pug was very cautious. As Jimmy the Greek observed, it's a very positional game, and on this one Pug had to feel his way gently.

"There's a possible straight out there. I've got to find out right here. Because I'm first, I've got to find out what's going on here. So I made a bet, to find out what's happening."

The next man called. "Naturally, *he's* not going to raise if he's got a straight. He wants us all in." Then the man behind called it. "*He's* not got the straight, because if he had, he'd bet it in that position. I don't know what's going on."

Fourth card up is another queen, giving Pug trips.

"Do you know how big my two queens were at the start?" Pug demanded. He raised his hand. "They were that big! And when that third queen fell, do you know how big they were then?" He squeezed his finger and thumb together. "That small! The queen is a perfect card for a straight if one of them came in with a jack-nine."

Pug, as first man to speak, checked. The betting went around to the last man, Crandall Addington, another Texan with an elegant air about his dress, fond of wearing a white trilby at the table. He looked good and he sounded good, and he put all his money in the pot. Addington is one of the few players who has had a college education, in accounting and economics. Poker is sublimation, he theorizes; after half a million years of men hunting one another, they now do it in a socially acceptable manner, at the poker table.

When Addington upped the pot, Pug was inclined to throw his trip queens in there and then. But as it happened, Addington didn't have enough money left to drive Pug out. "Everything is price-wise and percentage-wise, understan'?"

Addington did not have his straight but he was not exactly bluffing either. He had two nines in the hole. He reckoned he had two chances to win, in the sense that he could have bought the pot right there, or he could have improved after

Pug called him by catching a jack or a seven on the fifth card. The fifth card turned up low, however, so the three queens stood up. Exit Addington.

It is true, as Strauss said, that Pug learned hold 'em properly only a year or so before. That may seem surprising, but hold 'em, coming from Texas, had only recently come to be taken seriously among the big-money players in Vegas.

In the previous year's final of the poker championship Puggy had been beaten by Amarillo Slim. Slim, born Thomas Austin Preston, Jr., is much more a poker player's stereotype than is Puggy. He is tall and lean, wears cowboy boots and a Stetson, and is full of wise old saws.

One of his best, perhaps an explanation of what happens to losers in poker, is "Nobody knows where the hobo goes when it snows," delivered in a rich Texas drawl. Ask Slim if he wants a drink at the table and he'll say something like, "Us country hogs ain't used to city slops—bring me a glass of wa-a-ter, neighbor!" Slim likes to talk it up at the table. "Some of these guys play the games real uptight," he observes, "but Ah like to put a rattlesnake in their pocket and ask 'em for a match."

The crucial final hand of that championship (1972) went as follows. Puggy, dealing, found himself with 6-6 in the hole. He called the opening bet, Slim raised it well, and Puggy called. The flop came 8-8-K.

Puggy   (6 6)   8 8 K
Slim   (? ?)

Slim was first to bet and he moved in strongly. The pot was around $5,000 and that was what he bet. "Which he would do. I put him on two big cards in the hole, possibly an ace and a queen. He might have a king even. I don't know. But I know he's gonna bet that hand, regardless of whether he's got a king or not.

"So now once he's put the five thousand in, the pot's worth ten thousand. And I've got two sixes in the hole, eights and sixes. If he ain't got another pair with the eights, he's definitely got the worst of it. So I moved all in on him. And he had two kings." Puggy goes on ruefully, "I didn't know too much about the game then."

What would he do, now that he does know the game, having spent a year studying it very, very thoroughly. "What would I do, when a man raises me too much money, and I've got two sixes, and he comes out betting after the flop? I'd throw the hand away. What's two sixes? He might have two sevens in the hole! Might have two aces! He bet properly there; he bet the size of the pot. If he imagines he's got the best hand, you can't let a guy draw at you for nuthin'."

"Ol' Puggy jest had to go on and put his money in there" was Slim's verdict.

As it happened, there was more psychology to it than that. Slim had taken the measure of Puggy earlier, straddling every opening bet, regardless. If Pug opened $200, then Slim automatically bumped it to $400, before even looking at the hand he was dealt; and when Pug tried to take the initiative, by raising when it was Slim's turn to open, Slim socked it right back at him by raising to $800 in the dark, which meant he had stuck $1,000 in the pot without holding a thing.

Jimmy the Greek leaned over to Puggy and whispered that Slim was taking all the money without a hand. It was true, but it was not altogether helpful advice at that point. Slim (who likes to claim he is so sharp at the table that he can "hear an ant pee on cotton at two hundred paces") caught the remark. As he described the hand in his reminiscences, *Play Poker to Win* (written with Bill G. Cox, 1973), he made up his mind at that point: "The first time I make a hand—which I think is probably the winning hand—I'm going to sell it back to him real high, playing it just like the bluffs I've been taking him

with all along." Puggy at the same time was being egged on
to put a stop to all this straddling.

So when the flop came up 8-8-K and Slim found K-J in the
hole, he moved in. He knew that if Pug had a hand, he was
going to break him on it. There was $1,400 above the ante in
the pot, but instead of making a sensible bet, like $1,500 or
$2,000, which in a normal game he would fold if reraised, Slim
decided to stick it all in, $51,000. "It feels better in!" he hollers,
and the railbirds laugh with him.

Slim, using his knowledge to advantage, knew that Pug was
ready to call because of the bluffs he'd been taken on. With
his sixes wired in the hole, Pug didn't stall long, and called for
what he had left, $8,900. The next card up showed another
eight, which gave him a full house, eights and sixes. But Slim,
of course, was on to a cinch with a full house, eights and kings.

Slim became something of a national celebrity after winning
the championship. He had an engaging Texas style about him,
and gave the impression that he did not need the money all
that badly.

For instance, in a game elsewhere in Nevada, which lasted
seventeen hours, the big loser lost $312,000. "Ah ended up a
winner, but you could have stuck my winnings in a chigger's
eye and never seen 'em. It was 'bout nineteen thousand." Slim
has business interests in Texas, which means he doesn't *have*
to play poker for a living. Just as well, because Slim was
busted early in 1973's championship play by Strauss, before
Puggy could take his revenge.

Puggy has played an awful lot of cards in his forty-odd
years. He has, really, done nothing else in his life to speak of,
a realization that makes him sad at times, a feeling that if he
could have had a college education, if he could have traveled
some other route than the poker circuit around the United
States, he might have amounted to something. What? Just
something more worthwhile.

Pug was born in Kentucky in early 1929 to God-fearing people. It was a bad time to be born, what with the Depression about to set in. The family drifted south into Tennessee as his father followed odd jobs. As Jon Bradshaw recorded in *Playboy*, June 1973, they always moved on for the same reason: because the rent was due at dawn.

"There was never any money. They lived in the clapboard-and-log houses of the region, using coal oil for light, wood stoves for heat and cooking. The potatoes and whiskey were buried in the ground, the perishables were stored in the well house, the meat in the small smokehouse, and when there was fruit, it was dried and hung inside from the rafters. Times were hard and the nine children often went for days with nothing to eat but beans. Pug never saw a loaf of bread before he was ten."

His first day at school was an agony he still remembers acutely. " 'I had a complex about being poor and the shape of my nose. Everyone was better than me . . . I pee'd in my breeches that first day cos I didn't know how to ask to go to the toilet.' "

He left school at fourteen, having discovered where his talents lay. " 'I started hustlin' real young,' he recalled, 'at ten or eleven. I just started playin' cards and pool with the other paper boys.' " He traveled to nearby towns, playing pool, always on the lookout for action. ["Hustling" is strictly a complimentary term in Vegas; it means that a man knows how to look after himself. A tribute paid to one of the old-time gamblers: "He was still hustling like crazy at eighty-three."]

But it was not until he joined the Navy that Pug really started to play poker. " 'I learned the game real good. While everyone else was throwin' their money on drink and women I was organizing poker games and playin'.' "

When he got out, Pug got into his old car and followed the poker route around the country, a different game every night. " 'The boys could always count on me droppin' in on their little games. Knew I was comin'—same as Santa Claus.' "

Santa Claus hardly seems the right parallel, because Puggy was not coming down the chimney to distribute Christmas presents—quite the reverse. He got so good at poker that he could play with people who used marked cards and signals and still beat them every time.

Puggy played a lot of weird games on the road, for instance, the Georgia game known as *Get you one*.

It's a combination of gin rummy and poker, played by two players, the idea being to make a complete poker hand with your five cards.

After being dealt five cards, each player discards one card in turn, face up, and picks another one, either his opponent's discard or one from the deck.

When one player makes a pat hand of his five cards, he says, "Get you one," and his opponent then has a chance to draw one more card to fill his hand.

According to Puggy, it's a real simple game but a game of great skill. There is no ante; you play for so much a game. "Not only is git you one a good game but it's a good game for cheaters, too. They can hold out one with five cards; they can fix the deck, mark the colors; all they've got to do is make a quick poker hand."

Puggy will learn any game, no matter how way out, that can be played with a pack of cards.

At ease, in the cool living room of his home in Vegas, where he has lived with his family for more than ten years now, his little girl running in and out of the patio, Pug explained another thing: why players who knew how good he was were glad to play with him, and still are.

"I give them a square gamble." In a town and an industry

where all kinds of conning and thievery are habitual, instinc-
tive, and more or less ineradicable, Pug is one of those people
whose reputation is snow-white.

"I've had people come to me with propositions where I absolutely *had* to take somebody's money. But I just *could not*
go through with it. My mind just would not do it. And sometimes I could've used the money too!" Pug has not always won
all his life; like other professionals, he has been down and
out, and had to scrimp and scrape and hustle his way back
again.

"I'll tell you why," he goes on. "See, it don't make no difference how you do it. If you're going to steal the money, if
you're going to do something wrong—I learned this from the
old gamblers—don't make no difference how it is, sooner or
later it's gonna get out. And once it gets out—that you're a crook
or a thief or a cheater—if you're getting all the action in the
world, you're not gonna get it no more."

Winning at poker is quite the reverse process. "You can beat
a guy, just beat him and beat him and beat him, and he'll keep
coming back. You can just beat his brains out, knock him
down to the ground, and he'll keep coming back to get beat
some more. But you screw him out of one quarter and he'll
never come back!"

Cheating would not satisfy a real poker player, but, curiously enough, there is more satisfaction to the pro-cheaters to
cheat, even though they could take the money by fair play.
Someone's name is mentioned in this connection, someone who
got shot down the other day, which suggests that there are
more fundamental reasons why such a policy doesn't pay in
the long run.

There are three kinds of poker players in Vegas, it has been
well said. There are the cheats, the cheating gamblers, and
the professionals. The cheats won't play unless they can cheat,

the cheating gamblers will gamble even if they can't cheat, and the pros wind up with all the money in the end.

Pug insists that all the casinos run a legitimate business. They have so much capital invested, so many hundreds of millions, that they don't have any motive to cheat; on the contrary, they have good reason to keep the business clean. Besides, in Vegas, all the poker games have professional dealers, unlike Gardena, the gambling suburb of Los Angeles, where the deal rotates around the table.

Gardena is an undistinguished, unattractive location southwest of Los Angeles, where two or three poker palaces ply their trade (see Chapter Five). Various games are played for fairly low stakes and the house does its best to keep things straight.

But "teams" of players are working there all the time, Puggy warns. "If you get in the games where they're at, you can forget about winning. It would be an impossibility—an impossibility!—for a place like Gardena to operate poker games where there wasn't thievery going on.

"If the house breaks it up, what the hell, it's gonna come back again. All you can do—it's like cleaning your own house— is keep it clean; and soon as you've cleaned it, it's gonna get dirty again. Because people are gonna try to steal the money. You got a halo over your head, you're still gonna lose all your money!"

Pug has no trouble detecting cheating. "I can walk up to a game, I don't have to see nuthin' happen, I can see the people's faces. Not only can I see it, but I can *feel* it, when things ain't all right.

"Things just don't come up right! People have certain ways they play, and the more professional they are, the more they're gonna do it the right way. If things don't come up right, it stands out like a sore thumb. A good player sees bad plays, and he gets to thinkin', 'What the hell happened there? How did that play come up? This ain't r-i-i-i-ght!'"

Pug's aim at poker, his philosophy of the game, is to play what he calls a "fine line."

"You draw a line. Everythin' over on this side of the line is wrong and everythin' on this side is right. This is anything in life, doesn't matter what it is. The closer you can stay to this line, the more successful you're gonna be. Everybody else is gonna be fluctuatin' out in the right and wrong field."

This is why Pug prefers any form of limit poker (with seven card high his favorite game) as opposed to table stakes, the form of betting so often praised by small-time players who secretly consider themselves great gamblers. "In limit poker, if you get off the line you're not going to get hurt too badly. The best player's gonna get the money in limit poker, sooner or later.

"Say you have an ante of ten percent of the first bet from each player. Now then, that makes everybody get out there and play. They cain't wait for the nuts [cinch hands]. They've got to play, otherwise the ante will grind them up." Pug riffles a deck of cards to and fro with a satisfying snap. "Limit poker's like a slot machine. A slot machine's got a percentage going for it, hasn't it? Takes in a dollar, pays out eighty cents, eighty-five cents. When you're a limit poker player and you're the best player, at the end of a time period, the end of a day, the end of a week, you're gonna wind up with your end. Luck is always gonna break even. Everybody in the whole world is gonna get the same amount of luck."

If a man has an edge because he is the best player, then surely his return ought to be still greater if he is playing a no-limit game? Pug shakes his head vigorously.

"Maybe it is, depends how you look at it. But by the same token, if you're playing a *fine line* [you have to imagine that Tennessee rasp drawing out the vowels, fi-i-i-ne li-i-i-ne] and you get off kilt, you're in jeopardy, you jeopardize too much money, the sucker can pluck you off." That is, in limit poker, if you make a mistake and land on the wrong side of the line, the mistake is going to cost you only the limit of the bet, 10, 50, or 100 chips, depending on the limit of the stakes. But if you are playing table stakes, when all the money in front of you on the table can be bet, then one little mistake can cost you your whole bankroll.

Puggy illustrates his point from golf. (He is a great hustler at golf; billiards, too.) "Look, you and me go out and play golf and you're one stroke over nine holes better than me. You give me two strokes, and every time I get you two down, I let you press even. You don't give me one up on this next bit, we're gonna press even. We're gonna play every day, and every time I get you two down, you press.

"Sooner or later I'm gonna bust you! *You're* the best player, but I'm gonna bust you. You know why? Because when you get *me* two down, I'm gonna press. You're gonna win one bet. But the day you come out to the golf course and you're a little bit off, and I'm a little bit above my playing standard, I'm gonna drownd you that day. Because you're pressin', you're pressin', you're pressin'.

"Kickin' it up and doublin', I might win fifty bets off you. Do you know how long it would take you to win fifty bets off me at one bet a side of nine holes? That's what you call management. You can have the worst hand and be the worst player and take the money."

Puggy sums it all up crisply. "There are only two major things to gambling: that's knowing the sixty-forty end of a proposition and proper management—that's all.

"You can have ninety-nine percent the best of it, and if you've got ten dollars, a hundred dollars, a thousand dollars, a million dollars, and you bet it all, the guy that's got one percent going for him, he could win, couldn't he? But if you break it down into some kind of a spread, it's a lo-o-ong price that he's ever gonna win. When you're playin' limit, you're actin' like a businessman would do; you're showin' a profit all the way down. When it comes down to the end of the six months or a year, whenever you pay your taxes, you're gonna show some kind of a profit.

"And I've got too many obligations," Puggy goes on with a grin. "I've got my wife and my mother and nineteen animals. I've got to show a profit!"

This kind of approach to poker explains why the pros do not regard the Las Vegas world poker championship as a moneymaking operation. Certainly, Puggy came out miles ahead. He won the stakes of the finalists, worth $130,000, plus another $60,000 prize put up by the Horseshoe. But the general point of the championship was to attract publicity, bring the high rollers into town and create plenty of action.

It was a fantastic feat to win this event, because not only were all the players very good players, but the winner had to win *all* the money. If there is $130,000 involved, and you're $129,000 ahead, you still haven't won a quarter, as Puggy put it, until you've won that other $1,000. No wonder he doesn't like playing "freeze outs."

In fact, Johnny Moss had driven Puggy down to about $26,000 on two occasions in their final session. That meant that Moss was sitting on $104,000 in chips. But one of Puggy's best-developed skills is "stealing" antes, making aggressive opening or raising bets to drive the other player out and thus take the ante. At these stakes, when each ante was worth a minimum of $1,500, he was able by such means gradually to work himself back into the contest.

Moss had gone ahead on a couple of high, perhaps somewhat lucky, hands. On the first one, Puggy had found himself with J-Q in the hole.

Moss raised the pot; it came around to Strauss, who was still in the contest at this stage, and he called, and Puggy also called.

The flop came 5-J-Q. Moss had already raised the pot and gotten the others "involved." He then pushed all his chips into the pot. Strauss folded.

Puggy analyzed the possibilities. He had (J-Q)-5-J-Q and Moss with (?-?)-5-J-Q had raised the whole of his stack.

What's going on? "He ain't got three queens! He ain't got three jacks! He ain't got three fives! He ain't got two tens. He ain't got two nines. Only thing in the world that Moss can have in that hand is two kings or two aces. In case he catches somebody with a jack and a queen, he's still got an out."

It was, in Puggy's considered view, a very bad bet by Moss. He couldn't have three queens or jacks or fives, because no one would bet all his money on such a powerful hand and risk driving the other players out; with such a high hand, he would want the others *in* the pot. Two tens or two nines would be weak, against the jack and the queen showing. But Moss had to have something, and that something had to be aces or kings.

"I said, 'Well, Moss, you're gonna get some play! You've got two kings or two aces. I call!' "

The next card that came off was a blank, a deuce. Now at that stage, Puggy was a long odds-on winner. Moss had (A-A)-5-J-Q-2. As Puggy calculated it, Moss had eight "wins" left in the deck. That is, there were two aces that could improve his hand to three of a kind on the seventh card; or if another five or a deuce appeared, he could outdraw Puggy with aces up. If a queen or a jack showed, of course, it was Puggy who would win.

Puggy, sitting on (J-Q)-5-J-Q-2, didn't need to improve on the seventh card. He didn't need the four "wins" represented by catching another jack or queen; he was already best. More precisely, he had thirty-six "wins" going for him, the total number of cards (subtracting the hole cards and the up cards) left in the deck, less the eight that would help Moss. "You can figure precisely what the price is on it."

But as luck would have it, the last card to turn up was an ace—a chance of 22 to 1—and Moss took the money with three aces.

If the sixth card had been a five, giving Moss aces up, their positions would have been reversed. Puggy would have then had the extra insurance of his four wins on the last card—two jacks or two queens to outdraw—an 11 to 1 shot.

The next time Puggy faced a situation when Moss had put all his chips in, he had (J-2) against Moss with the board showing 2-J-8.

Next up card was a king. Here Moss bet his whole stack again, and Puggy read him as semibluffing the pot on two jacks.

Puggy   (J 2)
                    2 J 8 K
Moss   (J ?)

If so, there was only one card Moss could catch to win the pot—a card to pair his second hole card, which, as it happened, was a six. In exact terms, there were forty-four cards left in the deck, of which only the three remaining sixes would give Moss best hand, with jacks up. If another eight showed, they split the pot jacks and eights, with a king; and if another king showed, they split the pot kings and jacks, with an eight. Therefore, of the forty-four cards, there were thirty-five that would give Puggy the win, six that would tie, and three that would lose for him. Again, an odds-on position.

Puggy did not know that Moss had a blank in the hole, of course. He could have had an eight or a king. It was a clever bluff by Moss, but once Puggy called, he was set to lose. But Moss's luck was in again; he caught his six on the last card.

Yet Moss never quite looked like lifting the championship. Puggy kept climbing back, grabbing antes and small hands. After Moss failed to run his big bluff of a spade flush—the crucial hand described earlier—against Puggy's kings up, he seemed to wilt. That hand reversed their respective strengths, giving Puggy the lead with some $85,000 in chips against Moss's $45,000.

From then on, Puggy considered, it was only a matter of time, and as the clock crept on toward 4 a.m., Moss might have been wiser to request a break until later in the morning, as he was entitled to do. But the organizers wanted to wind up the championship that night if they could, and Moss played on.

The hand on which Puggy finally froze his challenger out was, nevertheless, a remarkable hand to play and a remarkably played hand.

Puggy was dealt (A ♠ 7 ♠), Moss dealing.

As usual the dealer had anted $500 in the pot and the second player $1,000. Moss opened with a standard bet of $1,000 which Pug just called. If he had had an ace and a seven off suit, he would probably have raised, to push Moss out. But an ace and a seven in the same suit is a strong hand at hold 'em. This was a hand Puggy wanted to play.

The board came 3 ♣ J ♠ Q ♠.

It was then Puggy who had to act first. He wanted first of all to find out if Moss had anything. In fact, he wanted Moss to raise him. He couldn't check, because he knew Moss well enough to know that if he had a big hand, he was going to check it too.

So Pug bet three chips, $1,500. At this point Moss could read him simply as trying to steal another ante. Moss raised, as Puggy had hoped he would. So he then raised back all Moss had left, the rest of his $45,000.

At this stage, with (A ♠ 7 ♠) 3 ♣ J♠ Q♠, Pug had no pair,

just a four flush and hopes from two cards to come. When Moss pushed his chips in to call the bet, Pug's hand looked weak. But that was not how he read the situation.

"The only way Johnny can have the best of it is to have two pairs or trips. He can't have the best of it any other way." But surely one pair is good enough against Pug's ace high? "No! He's got the worst hand with one pair. Supposing he's got a queen in the hole, giving him a pair of queens, he's still worst!"

Pug explains. With seven cards dealt, there were forty-five cards left in the deck. Of those forty-five, there were nine spades and three aces, all of which would win for him. He had two draws to catch one of these winning cards on the sixth and seventh up cards. That was twenty-four chances out of the forty-five cards, against twenty-one chances for Moss, *if* he actually had the pair of queens. So 24 to 21 is a little less than 6 to 5; in fact, you could lay 5½ to 5 or 5¾ to 5 and win the money.*

Supposing Moss had the pair, then a card to make two pairs wouldn't help him if it was a spade, because Pug would make his flush. That meant there were only two queens in the deck left to help and two other cards to hit his second hole card, a total of four wins, or five if his second card in the hole happened to be a spade. (If one of the other facing cards, the

* That was how Pug calculated it, but, in fact, the odds were not quite like that. For on his argument, if he had four draws at it, he would say it was better than a certainty—48 out of 45. The correct calculation is as follows.

The chance of the next (fourth up) card not yielding a winner is $\frac{33}{45}$. If this card is not a winner, the chance of the final card not yielding a winner is $\frac{32}{44}$. So the chance of not getting a winner on either draw is $\frac{33}{45} \times \frac{32}{44} = 0.533$. The odds of getting at least one winner are 0.466. That is, instead of being odds-on, it is 4.37 to 5.

Puggy's error was to forget that sometimes both draws would be a spade or an ace, but he won't win twice when this happens. But if his calculation of the odds was mistaken, his reading of the hand as a poker player was absolutely right, because his single ace was sufficient insurance.

3 ♣ or the J ♠, was paired by the fourth or fifth up cards, this would give both players a pair.)

What, in fact, was Moss playing on? With 3-J-Q showing, Pug read him (as it happened correctly) as trying to hit a straight with K-10 in the hole.

How good were his chances to improve on the sixth and seventh cards? He could hit three aces, or three nines (not the 9 ♠) for a straight: six wins.

He could pair up and win, on a king or a ten, provided they were not spades, which made another four cards to win. That meant that out of the forty-five cards left, thirty-five would win for Pug.

In the hush of Binion's Horseshoe (world's highest limit, as the ads claim), the dealer burned the top card, Vegas fashion, and turned up the next one: 6 ♦; burned the next top card and turned up the next one: 5 ♥. The single ace of spades was good.

Puggy   (A ♠ 7♠)
Moss   (K ♦ 10 ♥)   3 ♣ J ♠ Q ♠ 6 ♦ 5 ♥

"Gawd," breathed Pug, "I've done it."

If Moss had hit a pair on that last card and had won the pot, however, Puggy would still not have been finished. At this late hour it was he who was ahead in chips and who had set Moss in for all his stack. Puggy would still have had some $30,000 left in front of him to continue the struggle. And on his form then, most of the pros would have bet that he could have done it. Moss had his share of luck, but it was not his night. He took his defeat gracefully.

(What's more, Ol' Johnny was back next year to show his younger rivals a clean pair of heels. Puggy and Slim were knocked out early and dandy Crandall Addington, a generation younger, went down to Moss in the final.)

Pug's judgment, thinking it all over later, was that Moss should not have been in the hand. After Pug's heavy reraise on the flop, the chances were against Moss and he should have folded. Easy to see looking back; hard to read at the critical moment when the cards fell. Moss was certainly tired; he could plausibly take Puggy for, say, A-Q in the hole, and reckon that his own hand had three aces and four nines to improve to a straight, with two cards to come. He was in the mood, at that late hour, to stick it all in.

In this final session of the championship Puggy personally busted eleven of his twelve challengers, only one of them being put out by another player. Or rather, they busted themselves, because on each occasion it was some other player who bet all the chips he had on the table, and Puggy who had the onus of calling. The only times Puggy himself made a bet of all his chips, as in the final coup, he had the best hand.

After winning the championship, Pug gained twenty pounds and said his game went straight to hell.

CHAPTER FIVE

Breakfast in Vegas

The greatest advantage in gambling lies in not playing at all.
—Gerolamo Cardano (1501-1576)
Book on Games of Chance

On a sunny day, with nothing particular to do, an indulgent thought sometimes crosses my mind: *On the whole I'd rather be in Las Vegas.* Vulgar, eye-aching, money-grabbing Vegas, the place whose relentless tastelessness gives you the shudders. I love it.

As the plane banks over the glowing Sierra Nevada, sweeping past ridges and gulches and canyons, I crane in my seat for the first sight of the blaze of light of the downtown saloons, visible from the air even at noon, a pinpoint of colored light in the desert. At that first glimpse of the long, white highway that runs up to the Strip, with the straggle of mobile homes and cheap housing revealing another, tawdrier side to Vegas, my pulse beats faster, like the pilgrim sighting journey's end. McCarran airport, that transit point of broken hopes, where so many have arrived as would-be conquerors and fled with their tails between their legs, offers its own warning: you are made to walk such a surprisingly long way from disembarkation to the final arrival point. Why? So that the slot machines lined up along the route can tempt you to part with the first scoop of your small change. It's not chance; it's planned that way. Like everything else in town, the idea is to separate the visitor from his money, rapidly, efficiently, totally.

The first time I went to Vegas, as a freshman from Cambridge University, it was the usual story. The chicken was plucked. I had a "system" for roulette based on waiting for a certain number of reds or blacks to show in succession before doubling up (bright I wasn't) on the other color. Round about three in the morning, a sequence of fourteen reds wiped me out. I did catch Mae West's show, though, and that alone was more than worth the trip. At that time she had a troupe of Mr. Americas dressed in leopard-skin trunks and thigh-length cloaks. She had them standing around her in a semicircle, with their backs to the audience, who could see only the backs of their cloaks. Mae, spangled and statuesque, stood in the center of the group, facing it, eyeing each man up and down very slo-o-owly, giving a little satisfied "Mmmm!" as her limpid gaze paused at each male midriff. Her big number was "Frankie and Johnny," which she belted out as though this were the day of judgment.

I also played a little draw poker downtown, 10¢ ante and $2 raises. Dealt a low straight, I nervously asked the dealer, in my breathtaking English accent, if five cards in sequence was a good hand. Naturally, everyone folded, and I still remember his dry reply: "Cut yourself a piece of cake." Weak though my play was then, I saw that it was, in fact, possible to win money at poker in Vegas, though not this time. On arrival in Los Angeles by bus, I checked into the YMCA and asked for the cheapest room in the house. The receptionist handed me a key and observed "Another one in from Loss Vegas."

My favorite time of day in Vegas is breakfast.

The sun is booming down even at that early hour, or not usually so early when the gamblers awake. You feel the shock of hot desert air on your skin, against the artificial cool of the hotel-room air conditioning. The dazzling light half blinds you, strolling over from the cabana or motel before entering the dark of the coffee shop. Picking up one of the local papers, those smudgy prints of show reviews and nonevents, you slip into an empty booth and order orange juice and coffee. "Hi there!" The overpainted, overworked waitresses, with names like Leila and Dolores pinned to their bosoms, are trying to make the customers forget what happened the night before, and collect an extra quarter tip. The gamblers sip their coffee, mentally run over the remaining dollar bills in their wallets, figure out maybe it's not so bad after all. If the dice had just rolled a couple of times the other way, if they had doubled down a couple of times more, they would be back to almost even. *Yeah!* They take a second cup of coffee and begin to slide toward optimism.

For the poker player, as he digs into his eggs sunny-side up, there is the enticing prospect, the incredibly marvelous prospect, that he can eat his breakfast, saunter through the door, and whamm! there are one hundred games going on all over town just waiting for him, where he can find a seat open and sit down and play cards for as long as he cares or can afford, with none of the effort he has back home of ringing up the boys, prodding everyone to be on time, worrying whether John's check will be good or whether Jack will lose his temper, or keeping the wives happy, none of the hassle of getting the group together. Just sit down and deal!

And then, lazily to consider, where shall it be? To warm up with a little razz (seven card low) at the Stardust, where two or three tables are already getting into their midmorning stride, and three or four of the pros in gaudy beach shirts are noisily shooting the breeze in a corner, waiting for the high action; or to saunter up the Strip to the Aladdin, where a table of seven card stud will doubtless be under way; or perhaps go downtown to the sawdust-and-silver caverns of the Golden Nugget or the Four Queens and get pulled into a stead game of hold 'em. There is, indeed, the swimming pool, the country club, or even the bar; but such distractions are as far removed from the thoughts of the poker player at this hour as would be a course in motherhood to the hooker, already perched in the vicinity of the bar as brunch approaches.

Sit down and deal! It is not generally realized how much action at poker is going on in Vegas, or in Reno, for that matter, which is a homier town in the same life-style. The reason poker is overlooked is that the managements of the casinos want the vacationeers to gamble, and tempt them with slot machines, blackjack, craps, and roulette in unlimited abundance. At these games, the house must win, all the time. Poker is not a gambling game between the house and the players, but between the players themselves. The house makes a good profit from seat charges, and a poker table takes up very little floor space; but this is not what Vegas is about. The "legalized rip-off," as a California girl studying sociology once described it to me, is based on getting the folks all warmed up and excited around the gaming tables. The classic example of this policy is how, after the dinner shows with their cabaret stars, the diners can't get out of the place *except* by passing through the banks of tables and the serried ranks of croupiers, through the heady, hypnotizing clink of light and action. They simply *have* to gamble.

Would you believe a poker table makes a quarter of a million bucks a year for the management? It's possible you might have a table of nine seats, at $5 a head an hour, open around the clock, but let us say, by way of example, you have an average of seven players twenty hours a day throughout the year. The gross income will be $255,500. The return could be much higher than that, where the dealer cuts the pot; or if business is slack, it could be a little less. In any case, the only investment by the house is in a few decks of plastic cards and the dealers' salaries, which are modest. Why aren't the dealers making a living by playing poker themselves? Good question. Maybe they tried but discovered the hard way that a regular weekly wage plus tips made for a steadier life and kept their children better clothed. There are also "shills"—legal under Nevada law—house players who stick around to get games going when there aren't enough customers, but you can pick them out without asking the management (as you are entitled to do) who they are.

The question of whether the games are straight cannot be answered with an unequivocal yes. The point is, why should they not be, when the management can make so much money running a legitimate operation. At the same time, it is inevitable that cheats and sharks of one kind or another will be floating around, continually seeking to find ways of fixing the game—holding out cards, marking cards, working in teams, and any other device known to man for turning a dishonest dollar. The managements do their best, in the leading casinos, anyway, to detect and keep out such operators, to protect the ordinary player, but inevitably they will creep in. There's nothing new under the sun: crooked dice have been found in excavations of prehistoric graves all over the world, North America included. You need to be alert.

The main thing about poker in Vegas is to judge your man. You need to know who are the high rollers, leading a life of sporting retirement in the sunny West; who are the pros, sharpening their teeth on the passing trade; and who are the tourists, in and out of town on a convention or a five-day vacation.

Since everybody in the United States is likely to dress the same way, and a millionaire often looks like a shoe clerk, these distinctions may not be immediately apparent. But they show at the table. Who talks with whom? They seem awfully well acquainted, these deep-tanned guys joshing around. They know all the staff and pinch the bar girls' bottoms. They are "environment," part of the permanent scene. Most of them play well enough and none has survived in this town without a lot of loot. The tourists are easy to pick out. They are not relaxed as they count over their piles of chips; in fact, they are downright nervous, because this is not the Tuesday-night game in Gary, Indiana, but pok-uh at *Lahs* Vegas. Some of them play pretty well, despite inexperience, but they lack the essential ingredient of the pros and the permanent residents: stamina. For a while, especially because the regulars don't know how the newcomers play, haven't registered their values, the out-of-town boys may win. But time will take its toll. Four or eight or twelve hours later, when their alertness has become frayed, when they have taken that fatal couple of whiskey sours at the table, they are going to get clobbered.

As in golf, a weekend player may go out Saturday morning, hit a beautiful drive down the fairway, and chip the ball up to the hole as if it were a homing pigeon; but the club pro, who is on the course day after day, who can hit every shot in the book accurately nine times out of ten without even thinking about it, is going to wear the amateur down. It's just a matter of playing enough holes.

Accordingly, you need to find the right level of play to suit your style and your stakes. You are not, so we assume, clocking into Vegas just to play the tables and whoop it up around town. You are there to *win*. Winning here is the perfect example of what Vince Lombardi, the celebrated manager of the Green Bay Packers, meant when he once said that winning is not the important thing, it's the only thing. (If your wife understands you, she'll understand that too, and wait at the pool while you play.) When you have gotten ahead of the game, *then* is the time to have a night on the town, at the losers' expense.

So my recommendation is to start slowly. On a long weekend or a five-day trip—and even for us most dedicated Vegas lovers, a week at a time of its deathless vulgarity is about as much as we can take—start downtown in the nickel-and-dime draw games, where a $2 bet is the maximum. Play for an hour or two and win some small change. Then move up to the next game, say 50¢ ante and $5 raises. Take it slowly; this is just limbering up. Stop for lunch, have a nap or a swim or take in a show before the evening session, when you get down to the serious action. Move up to one of the hotels on the Strip and sit in on a bigger game, say $1 ante and $10 raises at seven card stud or $20 raises at seven card low. Play for a couple of hours, observing the company. One of the pleasures, perverse as it may be, of playing with strangers is that you don't have to be polite. Certainly you can make your little alliances at the table, chatting between deals with the farmer on your left, with his Stetson pushed back off his forehead, or with the sweetly smiling hard-as-nails lady to your right, probably an habituée—they each have something to tell you, about themselves or about the game; or you can be as curt as you like with the mean-looking unshaven guy across the table, check and raising him, or pulling in a pot with contemptuous confidence. Get to know the company, because in the next few days the seats around the table mark the horizon of your world.

It's dangerous to switch levels of play too quickly; you lose your balance, like a climber losing his footholds. I got caught that way one fine morning at the Stardust. We were playing a quiet game of seven card razz, $15 raises, with five or six players, warming up the table for the midmorning crowd. I was going on steadily, winning $100 or so, when four of the regular gamblers in the room drifted over. They were bronzed, affable, joking around, millionaires for all I knew, for they were talking about flying upstate in a private plane for some fishing together, and in a trice our friendly little $15-raise game was over and the four of them plus myself were playing seven card low at $100 raises. The other players, tourists, pushed their chairs back. In the second hand that was dealt I was outdrawn by a six-five low holding a seven, and it cost me

$750. A few minutes later the boys got bored and drifted off to check out the horse-racing card. I was stuck with my loss, which was out of all proportion to the original game I had been involved in. There was no chance of getting it back at $15 raises, and besides, the table had folded. My mistake wasn't in not catching the low hand. It was in getting involved in the first place.

The amount of money that you stake yourself with at Vegas is, obviously, a personal decision. The temptation to blow your entire bank balance is controlled, fortunately, by the sensible house rule that you cannot draw more chips than you originally arranged for when you were setting up your credit, and were of sound mind. That is the normal practice, but there are always ways of raising money, including (but definitely not to be recommended) a service for cashing out-of-town checks at an exorbitant discount. As the absolute minimum in any game, you need enough money on the table to stand a succession of three losing hands in which the betting goes all the way, which at seven card stud would mean fifteen times the basic bet; in practice, double that amount would be a reasonable starting stake; in draw, when there are only two betting intervals, ten or fifteen times the basic bet might be enough money. The essential point is that you can't play good poker if you are worried about your financial backup.

What's more, a towering pile of chips in front of you has an inhibiting effect upon the opposition, in addition to boosting your own morale. In short, take adequate funds to see you through a losing streak; and if your opening stake is wiped out in your first session, take a walk, have a coffee, change to another table. Take it easy. If on the other hand—and why not?—you are hit by a shower of good fortune straight away, there are plenty of banks where you can deposit your winnings.

My own record at Vegas has been moderate. I have won, including once paying for a complete vacation across the West,

and I have lost too. The losses, however, have almost all arisen
through lack of discipline by getting involved at blackjack.
You know, while waiting for your lady before dinner, or while
passing through the gaming tables, well wined and dined
after the show, you venture a couple of bets and then, annoyed at losing, you double up, and then . . . It's the old
story. One of the little catches about life in Vegas is that there
is nowhere you can sit down (apart from the men's room) to
relax or read a book. Nowhere! You have *got* to squander
money. The nearest approximation to an easy chair is found
in the lounges where keno (like bingo) is played. The numbers light up on the board every few minutes, as they are
called out by the fellow making the draw, and if you keep
your head down over your magazine, it's just possible you
won't be noticed and won't be badgered to buy a card.

Vegas is a run like a huge turbine, day and night, and you
can sense its tightly coiled power eveywhere you go. It is apparent in the watchfulness of the managers in the bull pens, in
their capacity to lean over their desks to check the accounts,
deal with customers who have queries, and at the same time
still watch the operation out of the corners of their eyes; it is
tangible in the strongrooms behind the cashiers' grilles, with
the cashboxes stacked up to the ceiling, three for each table,
covering the three shifts of the twenty-four hours; it is evident
in the legal wrangles and, occasionally, the shoot-ups that find
their way into the press. The "mob" is generally supposed to
be behind the Vegas operation. There have been many accounts describing how Mafia money is funneled into gambling
and other villainy; what is worth noticing is that whatever investment organized crime has in Vegas—and the link is not
seriously disputed—that investment is "legitimate," the money
is really made to work. For the poker player who is, properly
speaking, outside it all—not a unit on the conveyor belt of
Middle Americans being fleeced, but a player relying on his

own skill—Las Vegas has its uses and, undoubtedly, its attraction.

The same cannot be said of Gardena. This is a losers' town, but if you're stuck in Los Angeles on a hot night, when the restaurants are offering nothing but chile con carne and the movie houses nothing but third-rate sex films—why not? Admittedly, the suburb of Gardena is not one of Los Angeles' best features. It is nothing more than a desolate crossroads between the looping circuit of expressways, "a repository for exhausted lives," as playwright Jack Richardson once put it. But Gardena has a claim to fame. It is a place built up on, indeed, dedicated to, the playing of poker. The action takes place in three or four poker palaces next to the crossroads, large white halls, like *palais de danse,* run on a drab commercial formula but run quite successfully. A California law, which prohibited playing poker in public, incorporated in the statute only the term "stud poker," leaving a loophole through which some ingenious entrepreneurs in Gardena saw the chance of exploiting draw. So it is draw in a variety of forms that takes place inside the poker palaces, where, day and night, while there are five players to keep a game going, poker may be played by anyone who can put up the ante. The stakes are not high, going from 5¢ ante and $1 bets up to $20 raises, but they are sufficient.

The trouble with Gardena is that the poker palaces, with their metallic cleanliness, are totally lacking in atmosphere. You can forget those stories about picking up lonely and romantic housewives—the scene in Gardena is just too mechanical. Everyone is there to play, but the poker, too, lacks sparkle. On my first visit, I hit such a tremendous streak at five card draw lowball that no one could believe it, and I shot ahead several hundred dollars. One or two smart players at the table pushed their chairs back when they saw how hot I was and moved to other tables, but my luck turned as the hour grew

late. At three in the morning, squeezed between two Filipino-
Americans who were obviously working together as a partnership and raising me out of each hand, I had the sense to quit.
The most refreshing thing about Gardena is seeing the ocean
as you drive back to Los Angeles.

Whereas when leaving Las Vegas, I always feel a pang,
wondering how long it will be before I get a chance to come
back. Going out to the airport, the hands that I misplayed run
through my mind, over the banal chat of the taxi driver. He's
seen 'em come and, boy, he's seen 'em go. I remember the bad
bluffs, the bad calls, the sandbags I ran into. One hand often
gives me a rueful smile, not because there was so much money
at stake, but because it illustrates the unpredictability of
poker. I was involved in a very small game of seven card stud
at the Golden Nugget, sitting next to a birdlike old lady, sev-
enty years old if she was a day, and stoned out of her mind on
Old Fashioneds. The barman would occasionally bring her a
fresh drink, although she was so far gone that she could hardly
speak three consecutive words—"Ca' two dolla"—and could
not handle her chips at all. The dealer had to rake in the
counters for her, and once she actually fell forward with her
head across the table. This was around five o'clock in the afternoon, but the dealer didn't get someone to lead her gently
away, which would have been the kindest thing to do for her,
let alone the table, because, after all, the little old lady had
paid her table money to sit down and if she wanted to drink
herself into oblivion that was her affair. I finally got a hand,
three jacks wired, and bet it. The old lady, wobbling, peering
forward at the table, not seeing anything beyond her whiskey
tumbler, kept pushing her chips vaguely toward the pot, and
finally, in a rare gesture of coordination, more luck than de-
sign, managed to grasp hold of her hole cards and bring them
up to her face. In doing so, she showed the cards to me full
face for about ten seconds before finally raising the bet again.

She had something like Q-8 in the hole and was showing 9-3-2-10, no pair, no run, different suits. All right, madam, I thought, if you care to show your hand to all and sundry, who am I to look the other way. I bet, she raised, I reraised, and the last card was dealt. I did not improve three jacks and bet again. The old lady just managed to get out "Ra'," the dealer shoved her chips in for her, and I merely called—it did not seem right to go any further. And the little old lady, God bless her, had caught the case jack to make a straight. And at that point she careened slowly forward over the table once again and failed to move. They led her away, clutching her glass, with a man behind her carrying a whole hatful of silver dollars, which she had no means of telling were hers or mine or for that matter of belonging to the man in the moon.

McCarran on the way out is certainly a sadder place than on the way in. The tourists and trippers hurry down the long walk to the flight lounge, passing the slot machines by, untempted, purged even. The advertisements, with the razzle-dazzle suggestions of lights and gaiety and high action, mock the losers. Few are those who leave town as rich as the day they arrived. As the plane whines down the runway and lifts slowly into the desert sky, wheeling over the arid land beneath, you get the Las Vegas blues: "Next time I'll show 'em."

CHAPTER SIX

Loving and Losing

Sex is good but poker lasts longer.
—ALAN WILLIAMS

Has the excitement of poker something to do with sexual excitement? Well now . . . We play cards just for the helluvit, don't we? Still, it has a curiously compelling thrill, playing poker. It's like a series of tensions. Before the game, the tautness of anticipation. Everyone's on edge: will he, won't he, win tonight? During the game, the rapid kaleidoscope of hands, each of which may be fraught with risk. And then the end of the night, the winding down after winning or losing.

Then apart from the excitement, there's the time factor. Games go on a long, long time. Why? The first explanation that comes to mind is that the losers want to get even and the winners can't get out the door. Something in that, obviously. But still, poker is not a quick fling, as are roulette or craps or other casino games.

The idea that gambling has an intimate connection with sexual drives, certainly in its extreme form of compulsive or habitual gambling, is well established through psychoanalytic case histories. Poker is a game of skill, true; but there is a powerful gambling element within it. Presumably this is what keeps us going all night.

The rhythm is important, not just in the length of the game as a whole, but in the pattern of separate, constantly repeated plays that comprise it. As Ralph Greening noted in a psychoanalytic paper ("On Gambling," 1947), the atmosphere of excitement in gambling is visible in the trembling and sweating of players and in their restlessness, and is audible in the noise and the hushed silences. But that is only part of it. "There is a rhythm of tension-discharge, which is constantly repeated. At the beginning of play it is quiet, gradually there is a crescendo of excitement until a peak is reached, and finally there is a period of quiet. The excitement, the rhythm, the tension discharge, and the final quiet bear an obvious similarity to sexual excitement."

He was speaking of gambling games generally, but the description seems peculiarly apt to poker. On this analogy, the feeling of satisfaction or disappointment you get from winning or losing a hand is somewhat equivalent to having a good or a bad orgasm. Is that why games go on so long, a quest, in some oblique way, for the continuous or ultimate sexual fulfillment?

Poker players don't see it like that. Most of them claim to be studs, when the question of sex comes up. "You can score any time you feel like it, but a good poker game is hard to find," one player (a loser) observed engagingly, adapting the celebrated dictum that "a woman is only a woman, but a cigar's a damn good smoke." Notwithstanding such protestations, however, it would seem that if a man is totally exhausted after playing cards all night, he would not be inclined for a sexual bout the morning after, and that the purpose of playing all night might be, unconsciously, to tire himself out in order to evade a sexual relationship.

The theory fits, but players tend to scoff at it. The line is that after a good poker game, especially after winning, there is nothing more delightful than to drive home and jump into a warm bed. What about the lady whose gentle sleep is thus rudely disturbed? Has she any rights in the matter? Presumably she is simply supposed to be grateful that her man has come home again. Such an attitude goes with the *machismo* of poker, which makes it unique among betting games. Winning makes players feel more masculine. Only after a heavy loss will players admit that their potency is reduced: they're too depressed. But tiredness itself is no bar. "You see, the libido is entirely separate from your physical condition, even if you're completely exhausted," one player explained sagely. "That's the great thing about libido."

The *machismo* of poker is significant. It is the characteristic of the game. Both sexes play bridge together; among gambling games, both sexes play blackjack, roulette, or baccarat without any special attention being accorded to women; craps, with its noise and go-go atmosphere, is somewhat more of a male preserve. But poker, preeminently, is a man's game. Not that women are excluded, but the virtues of successful poker, which have colored the game since its earliest days, are the swashbuckling male qualities of courage, aggression, and bluff.

It would be surprising, this being so, if poker attracted players who are gay. It would seem that they would not be temperamentally disposed to enjoy it. But as in all matters sexual, motives are often the opposite of what they seem. In competing against other players, as distinct from an impersonal device like a roulette wheel, the other participants may serve various purposes in the unconscious fantasies of the neurotic gambler, Ralph Greening notes. Gambling with other men, he says, may be equivalent in the unconscious to comparing penises with other men; winning means having the largest penis or being more potent. In passive homosexual men, who love the type of man they would like to have been, contact with strong men in a game has the significance of gaining additional manhood. These comments refer to the neurotic gambler, whose psychopathology shows in a much clearer or more acute form attitudes which are "normal" to players in general.

Getting down to people's basic motivation is always a

lengthy process, and there is in the normal player no need for it. The masculinity of poker can be taken as an existential fact, arising from the kind of society we live in. Its masculine role may be enhanced or accentuated in these days of mechanical routine. On the one hand, at work, men find themselves increasingly dominated by technical decisions outside their control. On the other hand, at home, they are increasingly occupied with family commitments, as many are accepting the idea of sharing household obligations. Poker perhaps provides a healthy outlet for masculine aggressiveness, a chance for a man unabashedly to show his talents as a man.

The compulsive gambler is something else. The secret of his behavior is that unconsciously *he wants to lose*. The first explanation of this proposition was by Edmund Bergler, a one-time pupil of Freud's, elaborated in *The Psychology of Gambling* (1957). It seemed a startling idea at the time (though anticipated by Freud) but has since gained general recognition as an accepted psychological statement. Briefly, Bergler's thesis was as follows.

The neurotic gambler's real motivation is to punish himself for guilt feelings that derive from his earliest attitudes toward his parents. (As usual, everything goes back to the Oedipal relationship if you dig deep enough.) It's not that he ignores the laws of chance; he thinks he can overcome them, fortune will favor him, and he punishes his transgression against father or established authority by losing, which is indeed the point. Bergler sums it up thus: "In clinical terms, this is the psychic situation of the gambler: first, *unconscious aggression* [against parents]; second, an unconscious tendency toward *self-punishment* because of that aggression. The self-punishing factor, which is always present, is almost never recognized except in psychoanalytic treatment. Thus, the childlike, unconscious neurotic misunderstanding of the whole gambling process creates a vicious, and endless, circle. Hence the inner necessity to lose." Habitual gamblers can't stop—the most graphic example from literature is, of course, Dostoyevsky's *The Gambler*—although they "know" they can't win. They can't stop because they are in the grip of unconscious feelings which they cannot identify or control and which find their outlet in what Bergler called psychic masochism.

Losing is the name of the game. "I got a huge erection," a writer of my acquaintance, a man whose bisexual appetites were matched by wide scholarship, once confided, "when I was losing one night really heavily. It was a fairly small game, but suddenly I found myself getting into debt for an enormous sum, which I knew I could never pay. My excitement was something to do with the anxiety. In a dreadful way it was pleasurable. But then when I managed to win some of the money back, the excitement faded."

Not difficult to see in this surreal episode the typical experience of the habitual loser who actually enjoys his losing. In fact, this man corroborated it by recalling an incident from his childhood when anxiety induced sexual excitement. "As a small child, I was taking an exam, trying to answer the first question in the math paper on long division. I simply could not work it out, and I knew that until I'd done it I couldn't go on to any of the other questions. Time got shorter and shorter and I felt more and more desperate. I got an erection just like at cards." The gambler is like a naughty child who expects to be punished and gets a perverse thrill from that feeling. Bergler, describing an almost exactly similar case, says the sexual pleasure is repressed and unconscious only, though the above story would seem to contradict this contention.

The interesting thing about poker, which the psychoanalysts may not have altogether recognized, is that alone of gambling games, it comprises both kinds of player, the normal and the neurotic. I mean that everyone who plays roulette or craps or baccarat or slot machines *habitually* (blackjack may be an exception for the real pros), in a regular, addicted way, is, by definition, a gambler, and a gambler who *must* lose. The same goes, in almost all cases, for horse racing. The laws of chance and percentages will defeat them.

Playing the occasional game of roulette, or having the occasional bet at horse racing, is quite different; a flutter undertaken with full knowledge of the odds, in a spirit of adventure, is a way of spending leisure time.

In poker the two types exist side by side, the inveterate gambler and the player. The gambler, who is at the table to lose, although he may not know that is his unconscious motivation, is there to punish himself in some way; and the player, who is at the table to win by his own effort, to play a good game, is there for relaxation. (Compulsive winners may also be unbalanced, see Chapter Ten.) Habitual losers ignore the odds; they feel that they are above the laws of probability. They trust to luck, usually personified in the feminine as Lady Luck (who has some affinity with a rescuing mother figure, the analysts say). She is a will-o'-the-wisp deity forever beyond their call, for although sometimes she smiles upon them, in the long run she always spurns them. Since the odds are known to everyone and the books are all in the library, why should some players lose all the time unless they positively *want* to lose?

In between inveterate gamblers and players of skill, one may categorize a third type of player at poker, a character who alternates between them, who varies between gambling against the odds and playing according to the odds. This character resembles most of us. He knows what he should do but from time to time his emotions override his judgment and he gambles. One of the paradoxes of poker of course is that occasions often arise when a player should ignore the odds and play by some more inspired sense of values. Sometimes that is intuitive skill; sometimes it's the gambling instinct. Unlike gambling games as such, the dividing lines in poker are not clearly marked. When a regular winning player loses, he knows, even if he doesn't quite admit it, that he has been seduced into gambling (leaving aside outrageously unlucky cards). He may have been responding to some inner need or conflict and it may be that it was worth relieving his tensions by playing that way. A really self-aware player, perhaps recognizing in advance that his mood is edgy or that he is under some kind of strain, might have the resolution to miss the session altogether.

Gambling is pleasurable, in due proportion, and the nature of the excitement is illustrated by the word "play." All the analysts agree that gambling is a harking back to masturbation. Playing with the poker chips, counting them out, stacking them up, the smooth shapes and glistening colors, the sensual pleasure of handling the cards—"playing" the horses or "playing" the stock market, it's all of a piece. And why do you think that slot machines have to be operated by pulling a handle rather than by a simple push button?

In his study of Dostoyevsky, Freud pointed out the irresistible nature of the temptation to masturbate, the often-repeated promises to give it up, and the combination of pleasure as well as guilt feelings it induced. Exactly the same pattern is repeated in compulsive gambling.

"Lucky at cards, unlucky at love," as the old saying has it, is based on a more profound apprehension of a man's—or a woman's—attitude toward gambling than might at first appear. It means that the gambler is finding all the satisfaction he needs at cards and will have no time or energy left for relations with the opposite sex. This is above all true of the compulsive winner, who has no other interest in life except winning. But so far as the gambler is concerned, he is unlucky at cards *and* unlucky at love. He has to be, because the one follows from the other.

CLUB GIRLS

No girl I have ever seen at a poker table has ever managed to win consistently. There are plenty who try, in the gorgeous palaces of Las Vegas and in Gardena, and in the workaday casinos of London, too.

Women players, typically, are tense, beady-eyed, chain-smoking ladies, perched asymmetrically among the men, handbags between their feet under the table. There are exceptions, but on the whole they are a far cry from the languorous cuties you see displayed in casino ads. Is poker the last remaining man's game? That is not really a satisfactory explanation, because poker, being a game of skill, puts each and every player on his (or her) own, and sexual attributes don't, or shouldn't, enter into it.

The first ladies I ever played poker with were at Crockford's, that stately survival of a Victorian gaming club in Carlton House Terrace, London, S.W.1. It was a fine place, Crockford's, in the old days, before, like similar establishments everywhere else in London, it was turned into a casino. It used to be the home away from home of bridge players, and most of the England team played there. Going down the wide staircase to dinner, one would overhear intense conversations on the lines of ". . . so with no entry in dummy, of course I was squeezed, but if only . . ." which implied that there were as many hard-luck stories at bridge as at poker.

The poker room, on the top floor, was a remarkable sight. Some dozens of seven-sided card tables were filled with elderly ladies and gentlemen, with a high proportion of grandmothers among them, chattering, arguing, complaining, dealing the cards and throwing them in with machine-gun rapidity. My God, how fast they played! It was a club game in which each player around the table dealt a hand of draw, followed by three extra hands of deuces wild, misère (lowball), and draw or stud with wild cards. There was a blind and an overblind as antes, and fixed raises of ten shillings, a pound, or two pounds, depending on the game. And the reason they played so fast was to fit in one more hand—*one more hand, here you are, cut, deal!*—before the hour was up and they had to change around tables and pay another charge for the next hour.

Most of the old ladies played a terrific game, sharp, accurate, knowing the odds down to the last penny. When they weren't squabbling—"Open the windows, it's stifling in here." "Such drafts I don't need, thank you."—they were fun to play with. How their eyes gleamed when a new player, especially someone as youthful and green as I was, showed up. The first time I played was in the company of an aristocratic young sprig, Lord B, who, although a very good player, looked as fresh-faced as a pippin, and they couldn't believe their luck. They cut us up relentlessly. All those young boys' tricks at draw poker, like raising the pot and then standing pat with absolutely nothing in your hand, they were waiting for; all those hopeful raises after missing the one card draw to make a flush or a straight—smiling like crocodiles, they gobbled us up.

"What you should have done," an old club member told us later, "was on the very first pot raise and stand pat on a pair of deuces and then make sure you get seen. After that play every hand as tight as your maiden aunt." Lord B went on to speculate in the commodity markets, but I logged a good many hours at Crockford's and never quite mastered the old ladies.

It is, in practice, extremely difficult to win at such club games because the table money and the antes eat up your chips, and despite what some experts may say about the size of the game making no difference, the final bet is so low in proportion to the pot that you can't run your opponents out easily. Undoubtedly these club games require skill to win at. At Crockford's, for all the scores of senior citizens who milled through the poker room, only 7 percent ended up winners at the end of the year. What is more significant is that, year by year, they were the *same* 7 percent. Skill told. But the fast play was inhibiting and made the game too mechanical. I once asked mildly of a particularly sharp dowager across the table: "Did you bet two pounds?" "Yes, there it is!" "Oh, I see," I was murmuring reflectively when she pounced on my words. "You *see* do you! Three queens," and flipping over her hand, she raked in the pot. "Next deal!"

It is the table money, which seems so trifling at the time, that is killing. Most of the old ladies, with grown-up and married children and not much to do in the evenings, were playing a social game, and were prepared to pay for the pleasure. Anyone who paid £2 for the afternoon session, and £2 for the evening, plus another £1 for an hour after midnight, and did this seven days a week throughout the year—as very many people came close to doing—was paying £1,825 (or something over $5,000 in those days) for their pleasure annually. You had to get that back, with a maximum bet of £4 on the last card, just to break even, which shows the magnitude of the problem at club poker. Even social games cost money. Some of the old ladies got into financial trouble, but evidently found it worth it for the feeling of excitement. My own grandmother, who played poker in an earlier era, once remarked tartly, "I don't want to talk about it, dear, but I will say this: poker did get me through a very difficult time in my life."

There could be no greater contrast with the Crockford's ladies than the girls at the En Passant chess club in the Strand. This place, in its seediness somehow typically cockney, was more a way of life for its denizens than a rendezvous. Poker was played in a poky little cupboard of a room under the roof of an old tenement (now rebuilt, alas), one minute from the shops of the Strand but in reality as remote as a desert island. The chess, in a room below, attracted the usual crowd of Mittel-Europeans, would-be masters hustling cigarette money, and know-it-all kibitzers, but the poker (being marginally outside the law) was hidden away in the attic. The players who drifted in ranged from betting men and professional layabouts to printers from Fleet Street, short-order cooks from Soho, and on down to the occasional burglar. Sometimes they played for days on end and fell asleep in their seats.

Only two or three women ever played, among whom I became friendly with one, Jean. She was a dark, sloppy, rather attractive girl in her early twenties, vaguely working class, who had left home, and, most untypical for a girl at her age, was trying to make a living at poker. Jean sometimes won. She was popular with all the regular players, a kind of house kid sister, but she never looked happy even when winning. We had dinner together one night in Piccadilly, a meal that was worth its weight in gold to me, literally, because Jean knew everyone in the game and told me who the sharks were, who was cheating and how they did it. In that game even the cheats were not very expert at their trade.

Jean soon made it clear that whatever my intentions might be on the boy-girl level, her idea of how to pass the time after dinner was to return to the game. "You remember that hand of seven card?" she would exclaim, her forefinger stabbing at imaginary cards on the tablecloth. "I had king, queen in the hole, ten, jack. You were showing ace, nine. All right, next card gave you nines a pair. I got nothing. Now why didn't you raise? Next card nothing, nothing. You still didn't raise! Okay, last card. I buy the case nine to make the straight!" My fingers strayed over the tablecloth toward her hand. "How about coming back to my place, Jean?" "So what did you have, aces up? You should've bet 'em at the start!" "We'll have brandy and coffee there, shall we?" "Uh-huh." She pushed her chair away from the table. "Gotta get back."

Jean would put up a fiver, make it last through the night, go broke, borrow a couple of quid from someone she had done a good turn for the week before, and keep grafting. Winning for her wasn't really the point. Poker was a way of living, a refuge from the struggle of life with Mum in the suburbs, of working in an office as a secretary from nine till five, perhaps a defense against trying to find a suitable boy friend. The attic where the game was played, with its dingy, peeling walls and no windows, was a kind of womb. What mattered was staying in the game.

Lena was just the opposite type. A big, blowzy, cheerful lady of Greek origins, married to a secondhand dealer who seldom showed up, she wanted to win, seriously. Winning the odd pound or two meant the difference between keeping the children fed properly and going short. Lena wanted to win so badly that she couldn't really play poker; every time she was in on a hand where the chances were in her favor and she stood to win a sizable pot, she would make an offer to her opponent to split the kitty. This sometimes pays at hi-lo but is fatal at five card stud.

Lena might show (?)-10-J-10 against your (?)-Q-5-9, and fearful of a higher pair, she would try to make a deal, either not to bet on the final card or to "save" part of the pot for the loser. If she had bet the tens, she might occasionally have lost; but the odds were heavily in her favor that they would stand up. She didn't lose money this way, but she didn't make so much either. Poker is not a game where other players take pity on ladies in distress. If someone had the best hand against Lena, they usually kept betting. In the end she took a regular job somewhere and appeared only on Saturday nights.

LADIES' NIGHT

When a woman appears at the poker table, beware. She should be treated not as a man exactly, but as another player, strictly on the merits of her play. If some men like to behave chivalrously, that is their privilege, not mine. In any serious game, the lady will certainly be exploiting her gender—"sex" here is not the right term—to put the opposition off guard. A certain smile, a fluttering look, these are as much a part of a shrewd lady's technique as a calculated snub can be from a man trying to provoke the opposition. I like a little flirting at the table, just in case it puts her off *her* game. But cards are cards and bed is bed and seldom the twain can meet.

Have you noticed that when a woman sits in to kibitz behind a man, he usually plays badly? The distraction of having someone see your hole cards, the challenge to make an impression, can be fatal. If a lady appears, therefore, either at the table or in the room, the chemistry of the game is altered; a good player will turn it to his advantage.

Dear Lucia-Maria was one pretty lady who cost me money. At draw she had the infuriating habit of always buying only two cards to a pair and, so it seemed, always managing to hit threes or at least match her kicker. Since this draw is unsound and almost invariably unfavorable, I kept on chasing her and kept on losing. (By contrast, if she drew only one card, she was marked for trips.) She was as cold as an ice cube away from the poker table, and I realized later that her warm play was a way of seeking the attention she did not know how to attract as a woman. Anyway, one night when I was dealt three aces I announced that since her system was proving so effective, I would try the same technique and draw just two cards; and of course that time she hit a full house. In the end her loose play caught up with her, but Lucia-Maria had something extra in her hand: she upped and married a Spanish nobleman.

Sex and poker don't go together. That, at least, is my general experience. Which is not to say that one should not follow the other. But there is a major difference in the way the sexes approach poker. Young men come to poker as if it were an initiation rite in an Indian tribe. The game is a test that they face at eighteen or twenty, at college or on a night out with the boys, a form of social puberty. Poker challenges their masculinity, like running before the bulls at Pamplona à la Hemingway. Girls don't fit in. There are often girls around, but a girl's fate is to sit on the fringe of the action waiting for her man to finish the game, which inevitably means waiting up half the night. By that time the girl is just about dropping with fatigue and looking like last week's laundry.

Why don't the girls join in the game? Wha-a-t? A girl in a poker game? You must be out of your mind. This is a *man's* game! Any fellow in his late teens sitting around the kitchen table (covered with a blanket in place of green baize), riffling the deck (like the pro he remembers from a cowboy movie), has at the back of his mind a romantic image of Mississippi steamboats, impassive gamblers, and lightning gunslingers. That is the *machismo* of poker. Oh, yes, there is a place for girls. To watch and admire, and, still more important, *be* admired by the others. Perhaps the subordinate role assigned to girls makes poker the last refuge of male chauvinism. The man shows off his girl to his friends at a poker game. She watches wide-eyed and breathless as he coolly plays his cards and raises the betting. He is more than just one up on his fellows. He has proved his masculinity before a single hand is dealt.

Here is some sound advice to any woman who finds her man getting involved in a poker game. Have a drink, wish him

luck, and go home to bed. Resist all blandishments to the effect: (a) Why don't you watch the game for a bit? You can
learn how to play! (b) We're quitting at eleven-thirty. Why
don't you wait for me? (c) Will you sit behind my chair? You
bring me luck! (d) Will you be an angel and cook some breakfast for us? (e) Where did you get those beautiful blue eyes?
The answers to such questions can all be reduced to the same
basic formula: the fair damozel will be up very late into the
night, feeling increasingly bored and looking decreasingly
lovely. The books on etiquette may not say so, but the right
reply for a lady to all such advances is to smile sweetly and
say to her companion: "You win a lot of money and I'll help
you celebrate tomorrow." Any man will appreciate his girl
bowing out this way. If he does win that night, he will feel all
the better disposed toward her; if he does not win, he won't
have the humiliation of having her watch him losing his
marbles.

There are limits to this female chivalry, of course. If a man
wants to play poker every night, without any interlude for
dalliance, any self-respecting woman would rapidly conclude
the game is not worth the candle, and leave him. I know a foreign correspondent who, after spending forty-seven days covering war and revolution in the Middle East, celebrated his
getting back to base in New York by playing poker seven
nights in a row, whereupon his wife packed her bags and took
off for Florida to return to Mother. It took him another three
weeks and a tour of the Caribbean to persuade her to come
home again. My own rule, which was instituted some little
time before becoming officially engaged, is as follows: One
night a week it is decreed that all domestic arrangements give
way to poker, the only stipulation being that I get back by
breakfast. That's it. No second inning. Well, okay, sometimes
you just *have* to play another night because the boys need another player . . . You know how it is, don't you?

Despite an increasingly competitive society, girls do not seem to have the same need as men to assert themselves over one another. "A night out with the girls" has no ring to it. The fundamental reason, I think, why girls don't play poker, or don't play it very well, is that there is something *unsexing* about gambling games. To win, a woman has in some direct way to deny her femininity, to be hard, cunning, and aggressive; whereas for a man, poker reinforces his masculinity: he feels tougher and more sure of himself after winning. There are exceptions, like "Poker Alice," whose story follows, but they are rare.

FIRST LADY

Poker Alice, who made a name for herself as a poker player in the 1870's in the mining camps and shanty settlements of the Wild West, may be regarded as the first lady of poker. Pictures of her show a tough little old lady with a level gaze, something like W. C. Fields without any of the smirk. She was born Alice Ivers in England in 1851. The family emigrated to the United States, where Alice was given a Southern belle's education, and then moved west to Colorado. In her twenties she met and married a mining engineer out in Lake City, Colorado, one of the boom towns for miners. "The click of the poker chips across green clothed tables, the shuffling of cards all made a persistent staccato sound throughout the entire night," says Nolie Mumie's perceptive memoir of Alice (1951). Alice's husband died when a dynamite charge misfired, and Alice, who had already shown a liking and a talent for cards, was faced with the necessity of making a living.

" 'We were all gamblers in those days,' " Alice recalled. " 'Some staked theirs in mines, some in goods, some in cattle, and some with a pan on the streams.' " Alice sported long black cigars when she played, and never lost her clipped British accent. " 'You see, a true gambler played because he loved the thrill he had on the turn of a card, because it tested his ability to out-wit and out-guess the other person.' "

A woman gambler at that time wore long ballroom skirts, kept in tune with fashions, and was always well groomed. It is clear enough what kind of player she was: the hardest to beat. "She had the faculty of sitting at a table, gambling for hours with an expressionless face, regardless of the kind of hand she held." Asked if she ever lost much, Alice replied: " 'I've never seen anyone grow humpbacked carrying away the money they won from me.' "

Alice's life as a card player was distinguished by several exceptional qualities. She had courage; she had humor; she put life before gambling, and dearly loved her second husband. Gambling was in no way a substitute for living for Alice, and to the end of her days she remained a religious woman, refusing to work on Sundays.

Her sharp and stalwart attitude toward gambling is nicely illustrated in this story from Silver City, New Mexico.

"Alice entered a gambling hall, watched the faro game, placed a bet and won. She won again and again, and was soon betting the limit, which was twenty-five dollars. Onlookers began to gather around the table where she was playing. They were eagerly watching with intense interest the woman gambler who was playing the limit of the house. The cards were favorable, then again unfavorable, but her luck and skill continued to increase her winnings. The dealer became nervous. Never had he played against such a cool, determined player, who forced the game on and on until he finally turned his palms down and said, 'The bank is broke.'

"Alice, with grace and deliberate ease, walked around the table and took the dealer's chair.

" 'The bank is open, the sky is the limit,' she said."

Faro was the great game in those frontier saloons. It went like this: The bank dealt cards out of a box two at a time. If the first card matched the bets laid out on the board, where a suit from ace down to deuce was displayed for players to mark their bets, the player won; if the second card matched any bets, the bank won. When the two cards were the same, the bank took half the stake, rather like zero at roulette. This gave the banker an edge of about 3 percent, but often considerably more, depending, as in blackjack, on how attentive the players were. The temptation for the bank to cheat, by fixing the cards, was enormous.

Alice played a straight game. " 'The games were nearly always on the square; it was a matter of percentage and depended on the skill of the gambler,' " she said. According to *Faro Exposed, or The Gambler and His Prey*, a useful little book published by the proprietor of the *Police Gazette* of New York in 1882, "All regular faro players are reduced to poverty, while dealers and bankers who do not play against the game amass large fortunes; and again the higher order of faro-rooms are gorgeously furnished—luxurious suppers and costly wines are gratuitously given to players and the proprietors are everywhere distinguished by their reckless extravagance." Wise words! Which explain in our own times why casino owners drive home in Rolls-Royces, while the rest of us wait on the sidewalk for a taxi or plunge into the subway.

This account of faro adds another warning which shows that in this department times don't change much. "Almost every player has some peculiar system, which he strives to believe will beat the bank and which does sometimes realize his hopes. In the end all systems fail."

It was not easy running the bank at faro. The dealer had to watch the bets, keep an eye on the players, pay out and collect, and insure that the game kept moving smoothly. Alice was a professional. Working in Deadwood, South Dakota, she became known as Poker Alice. It was here, dealing faro at a table next to W. G. Tubbs, a rival gambler, that competition became so keen it became a source of hatred; they refused to speak to each other during their shift. Yes . . . you might have guessed it. Their jealousy ripened into a love affair, which led to marriage. Alice and her husband retired from the gambling scene to a homestead in the sticks at Sturgis, South Dakota, quite happy to lead a domestic life and forget the tables. This was probably the happiest period of Alice's life. When her husband died of pneumonia in 1910, it was a grievous loss. She had to pawn her wedding ring to meet the funeral expenses, and then returned to deal at the faro table to earn the $25 she needed to redeem the ring.

There were few women gamblers in those days, Alice recalled, because women had too many nerves. There were too many temptations which made them display their emotions— " 'feminine instinct prohibits the usual poker face.' " Alice believed that " 'one must have a countenance that can remain immovable hour after hour.' " She could also handle a gun. " 'I always carried a gun; it was .38 or .45 frame. You see, my father was an expert marksman. He taught me how to shoot, and to shoot well.' " She had to draw her gun only a few times in her career. " 'One time was when another gambler attacked my husband with a knife. I shot him in the arm and ended the quarrel.' "

Alice's style is shown to advantage by another incident at faro.

"I was playing faro and I had lost nearly fifteen hundred dollars and could not understand why I was always losing; so I began watching the dealer handle the box. I detected a crooked maneuver, and knew there was something wrong. I watched him turn out the cards a second time and he very clumsily handled it in a crooked way. Then I drew my gun. I said, 'If you'd have done that cleverly I wouldn't kick. I could admire a clever crook I'll admit that, but I have no use for a clumsy crook like yourself. Now before I pull the trigger, you give me back all the money I lost in your crooked dealing. I want all of it.'"

She got every cent of it back and walked out.

On the subject of guns, Alice also remembered a pretty girl called "Prairie Rose" who won a $50 bet that she couldn't walk down the main street of a Kansas frontier town without any clothes on. She picked a time when nearly everyone was off the streets, and took her walk with a revolver in each hand to discourage the peepers. After this, she was given the title "Lady Godiva of the Plains." "Faro Nell" was another good shot. " 'She could shoot a glass of whiskey out of a man's hand a few yards away, or the heel off his boots. She did shoot a heel off occasionally.'"

Alice's third marriage was typical of her down-to-earth approach to gaming. There was a fellow called George Huckert who ran her errands for her and fetched supplies for her in Sturgis. He often asked her to marry him, but Alice was not interested. She was loyal to the memory of Tubbs. But then one day she changed her mind about her suitor. " 'I know I owed him $1,000 and all I had was about $50 in hand. I got to figuring it would be cheaper to marry him than to pay him off.'"

When Alice survived this third husband, she resumed the name of Tubbs, the man she really loved. Her old age was somewhat troubled by harassment by the authorities, who seemed to think she was running a disorderly house. There was a brawl at her home in which she shot a soldier. There were a lot of good-time girls about, especially in the faro games, just as there are in casinos today, and it was up to the girls what they did with the men they met. From what we know about Alice, it seems unlikely she was a madam. Anyway, she always impressed on the girls the need for religion on Sundays.

Alice pleaded self-defense at the trial, and when she was acquitted, the townspeople were so elated they declared a holiday. In the end, Alice turned more and more to the Bible, and the soldiers at Fort Meade began to call her "Mother." At seventy-four, she remarked, " 'At my age I suppose I should be knitting. I would rather play poker with five or six experts . . .' " At seventy-nine, she faced a serious operation, knowing it was doubtful she would recover. " 'Go ahead,' " said Alice. " 'I've bucked worse odds than that, and I've always hated a piker.' "

The first clause of her will asked for a decent burial by the church. The second stated: "I hereby specifically disinherit each and every one of my relatives and kin, for the reason that they have not contributed to my welfare and happiness during the declining years of my life, nor have they made any effort to inquire as to my welfare for a great number of years."

True to the end!

CHAPTER SEVEN

Movies

All right, Nosy Parker—ace! I hope that satisfies your morbid curiosity.

W. C. Fields as Cuthbert J. Twilly
in *My Little Chickadee* (1940)

The best film about poker, curiously enough, isn't about poker at all. It's *The Hustler* (1961), which is about pool players. Poker in movies never quite comes off. It is, of course, a staple ingredient of Westerns—the dark saloon, with its gleam of glass and bottles behind the long bar; the bevy of blondes in high boots and lacy blouses, sidling through the throng of cowboys and gunslingers. The Western scene would be incomplete without a game of poker somewhere in the background. And sometimes a deal or two figures in the plot, with the hero exposing a cheater or staring down one of the bad guys in a big hand.

But the game itself is not usually observed in close-up as the primary interest. It is difficult to film a poker game because real-life play depends on a long series of hands, of dealing and chucking in, in which the action is repetitive and muted. The drama is an interior one, consisting of what goes on in the players' minds. The big hand, when it finally comes up in a movie, doesn't seem as thrilling as it should, shorn of the rest of the play around it.

An exception was *The Cincinnati Kid* (1965), which dealt with poker in an extended way. At the climax, Lancey Howard, "the Man," played by Edward G. Robinson, finally busts his challenger, the Kid, played by Steve McQueen, in a huge hand of five card stud.

157

It's one hell of a hand, all right—a straight flush against a full house queens at five card stud—and from the purist's point of view, it's just too implausible to make poker sense (see Chapter One).

But what is pleasing about *The Cincinnati Kid* is the myth it embodies, which reflects a deep belief of American life, the myth that there is one man, the champion, who reigns supreme at his chosen sport and that everyone else measures his own prowess against him. In this story, the Kid is out to challenge the champion; his whole life is being shaped to this one great tilt, to become the Man himself. The theme is given in the opening sequence before the credits come up, when a black shoeshine boy challenges the Kid to pitch coins against a wall, a contest they have played many times over. As usual, the Kid wins. " 'You ain't ready for me, boy,' " he tells his disconsolate young challenger. The question is: Is the Kid himself ready to take on Lancey at five card stud?

Opinion among the pros is divided. The Kid is good, very good; but Lancey hasn't been beaten since way back. There are some hands played early in the film, in one of which Lancey delivers himself of an immortal line. How the hell did Lancey make a big bet with no pair, the losing player demands, amazed at his downfall. Lancey, unblinking, scoops up the dollar bills: " 'All you pay is the looking price. Lessons are extra.' "

Lancey, played by Robinson with narrow-eyed impassivity, is a courtly, stylish old boy, and his whole character has a Deep South, almost eighteenth-century, air of elegance about it. He is quite right in observing that " 'for the true gambler, money is never an end in itself. It's a tool, like language to thought.' " But it is the high stakes, nonetheless, that give the challenge its intensity.

The problem of making Richard Jessup's little book into a feature film was simply that poker itself is not very interesting

Steve McQueen in *The Cincinnati Kid*

to watch unless you are directly involved in all its intricacies. The solution, which Ring Lardner, Jr., and Terry Southern devised, was to introduce a second theme, that of cheating.

One of the other players around town, a rich young sprig, ev'ry inch a fine Southern gen'lman, wants to take his revenge for his losses at poker against Lancey. It's not the money, suh, it's a gut feelin'. So he leans on the dealer who is hired for the big game to give the Kid an occasional helpin' hand. This episode is quite entertaining in Terry Southern's high-parody style, and, of course, the Kid spots what is going on, confronts the dealer, and puts a stop to it. He wants to beat the Man on his own merits.

And he would've done it, too, on the evidence of their head-to-head match. The Kid keeps on winning good hands against Lancey, who is evidently beginning to feel his age as the contest goes on. The Kid's judgment is clearer, his play is sharper, he seems to have the edge.

The portrayal of the game, though, hardly begins to suggest the true skills of poker, the stamina, the concentration, the gradations of daring, that really make for winning and losing in this class.

The final hand, when it is dealt out, depends on the extremely remote possibility of Lancey drawing a straight flush, starting with (J ♦)-8 ♦ * and reflects merely a fluke situation, not any real difference in quality in the two players' skills. It busts the Kid, though, and as he stumbles outside, past the jeers and cheers of the onlookers, he finds his young friend, the shoeshine boy, out on the road. The boy persuades the Kid to play their old game of pitching coins against the wall once more, and this time, of course, he wins. It's his turn to mock: " 'You ain't ready for me, Cincinnati Kid!' "

---

* The movie version is slightly different from the book (see pages 26-28) and, among other things, changes the suit from hearts to diamonds.

It's not a convincing ending, and in a different way the same goes for the poker climax in *A Big Hand for the Little Lady* (1966). Though this whole story is a spoof, it just about gets by thanks to the presence of Henry Fonda. He plays the role of a simple family man who happens to be passing through Laredo when the annual high-stakes poker game is on. The game is such a special event that the players have galloped in from far and wide, leaving wives and children at a moment's notice in their eagerness to get there. Fonda, a weak man, sees the game, is tempted to play, and rapidly gets in over his head for all his money. " 'The first rule of poker, whether you play western or eastern rules, is put up or shut up!' " Result: ruin.

Then comes the hand of draw when, picking up his cards slowly one by one, his eyes widen, his face pales, and his hands tremble at what he sees. This is the hand of a lifetime, but before he can play it and redeem his failure and his fortune, he keels over with a heart attack. In steps his lovely wife, who earlier had tried so hard to keep him away from the game, Joanne Woodward.

She is going to play the hand for him, she announces. Protests all around. She knows so little about poker that she even has to ask how they play the game. More ructions. Undeterred by the male ribaldry and protests, she gets her way. But first, she has to raise some cash to bet this wonderful hand.

She leaves the table, clutching her cards to her pretty bosom, and finds the local bank manager. Impossible! But when he sees the cards, it's another story; he agrees to put up the cash. The little lady returns to the table, and lays it all on the line. Stunned by the flinthearted bank manager's willingness to take her poker hand as collateral for so much money— " 'Sam,' " the boss orders sternly, " 'bring some chips in here!' " —the gamblers are convinced it really is unbeatable. They fold. And she sweeps up the pot.

What did she have? Nuthin', pardner. The whole thing was a con job, including Henry's heart attack. The bank manager was in on it from the start, and they all clean up.

The film ends with a nice touch, as Joanne Woodward, eyes aglitter, Henry in the seat next to her, riffles through a deck with a professional card player's *swoosh,* to get a real game going down in the saloon. Personally I found that one brief shot at the end better than the rest of the rather silly story that preceded it.

Poker as depicted in Westerns is not really about poker at all: it is an aspect of *machismo,* of being a man. The game is a way of showing character in action. The leisure time of cowboys, as it comes across in Westerns, was devoted to drinking, whoring, fighting, and playing poker, observes Philip French in his essay "Westerns" (1973). "All of them are essentially male pursuits, and the only one which does not more or less correspond to some specific physical need is poker."

This interesting comment is followed by a somewhat less perceptive remark that in the scale of card games poker stands near the bottom rung, a bit above faro. Since the author is a film critic, not a player, we'll let that pass, but his general point is surely correct: that poker is in some way central to the Western mystique. In the Wyatt Earp—Doc Holliday films, French notes that the hero must be capable of acquitting himself well at the gaming table as proof of his manhood. At the same time, he has to keep his cool and view the game almost dispassionately; he is not really involved. Henry Fonda exemplifies this attitude as Wyatt Earp in *My Darling Clementine* (1946). " 'Sir, I really like poker,' " he declares, " 'every hand has its different problems,' " but his own quality is shown not by his play but in the way he deals with a cheat. Unlike real life, cheats always come to a bad end in these movies, but then the traditional Western is a very moral kind of fable.

In fact, the poker game symbolizes, sums up in miniature,

as it were, the whole Western genre. Here across the table you have the good guy and the bad guy, facing each other down over the cards, the classic duel of individuals, which is what the old Western stories were all about. One false move, one rash accusation, and all hell breaks out. (Maybe in the better-class saloons, card players handed in their gun belts before taking a seat.) Violence is always close to hand and the play of the cards is of marginal importance compared with the interplay of character.

Masculinity, in a different guise, was still the underlying theme in movies of the mid-70's when gambling began to be treated as an aspect of living, like, say, *haute cuisine*, of interest for its own sake. Take *The Sting* and *California Split*, which were "male bonding" films. The essential characteristic was not the play, as such, but the male relationship it embodied, a kind of *machismo* in reverse. The aim was not to demonstrate manliness, but to color a buddy-buddy relationship and romanticize it. So far as women are concerned, they are irrelevant, decorative adjuncts to the male partnership.

Granted, there is a very good poker scene in *The Sting* (1973), in which Paul Newman gets himself invited to play against the villain on board a train. He knows the bad guy is going to cheat, but he is a better cheat, and switches the deck himself. In the big hand, the villain confidently announces, in his sly Irish brogue, four nines, but Newman with a light smile lays down four jacks. The joke of this confrontation is pointed up by the look of absolute astonishment on the face of the gangster's sidekick, watching the game from behind Newman's shoulder, when the four jacks appear from thin air. The cheater is outcheated: that's "the sting."

California Split (1974) is the ultimate in buddy-buddy pictures. The two heroes, George Segal and Elliott Gould, are more or less addicted gamblers—horse racing is their first love—and the gaming scenes have, unusually, the stamp of au-

Paul Newman in *The Sting*

thenticity on them. "No casino is going to shut down for even
five minutes to let a movie company shoot," explained director
Robert Altman. "It's too expensive for them. But, by placing
the actors in a realistic casino in a real gambling town, we
were able to create the atmosphere and stimuli."

The sequence at the tables in Reno and, beautifully done, a
poker game in Gardena, where Gould finds himself stuck at a
table of frowsty and argumentative hausfraus, have rhythm
and excitement. The director got some of the local poker players to sit in for the high poker game in Reno, Amarillo Slim
among them. It's all very pretty and there are no moral judgments. But over all, what counts is the thing going between
the two men, their link with each other, notwithstanding the
presence in the film of a couple of good-time girls who go
along for the ride.

Certainly the poker is not to be taken seriously. Segal, who
sits down with the hard-faced pros and wins, would not in real
life have had a ghost of a chance against them. He is a gambler who loves to gamble, who plays his streak when he's feeling hot—and why not?—but he's not a card player. The au-
thentic poker film is still to come.

Which takes us back to *The Hustler*. It has become a classic, and deservedly so. Though it's about pool, not poker, what
it's really about is winning and losing. It says it all and says it
well.

It's the story of a pool hustler, Fast Eddie, played by Paul
Newman. In the opening shot he is seen arriving at a two-bit
bar, accompanied by his pal, Charlie (Myron McCormick), an
older man, setting up one of their well-tried cons. Fast Eddie
has a few drinks, plays Charlie at pool, starts losing, pretends
to get drunk, and finally pulls off a terrific carom shot that runs
the ball back along the edge of the cushion smack into the
corner pocket. A fluke! But what a fluke!

" 'You couldn't play that shot again in a million years!' " says

Charlie disgustedly. " 'I couldn't, ha? Okay, set 'em up the way they were before . . . Bet ya twenty bucks.' " And of course this time he misses, incredibly badly, and the ball skews off the table. The locals guffaw. Fast Eddie is drunkenly resentful. " 'Set 'em up again,' " he orders curtly. Charlie doesn't want to bet again; they have to hit the road, he says, backing out. Fast Eddie insists, slamming his money down on the table. He wants another shot at it, right now!

The barkeep has been watching. He'll take the bet, he declares eagerly.

Eddie's eyes flash: the sucker's taking the hook!

" 'Don't bet any more money on the dam' fool shot,' " Charlie warns his pal, putting the hook in deeper, and stalks toward the door. He can't bear to see his friend throw it away. The barman fetches $100 from the till and lays it on the table. Then the *coup de grâce*. Looking down with a contemptuous glance, Eddie slams the ball into the pocket, whips the money off the table, and is out of the bar, all in the same sweeping motion.

Nice work. Accurate too, because it is the *greed* of the sucker that makes the hustler's skill pay. Without the victim's desire to get rich quick, the hustler couldn't con him along.

Fast Eddie and Charlie are after bigger things than conning local yokels out of their petty cash. They are heading for Ames's saloon, the mecca of pool players, the place where the men really shoot pool, the place where Minnesota Fats holds court over all comers. Here the story enters its mythic element, the theme of the player who has to prove himself by beating the best man in the country at his game, just like the Cincinnati Kid playing the Man at stud. The boy comes into town, he's out to challenge the master, he gets down to playing head to head, and then . . .

In *The Hustler*, this theme is elaborated with compelling force, not only in the strong acting by all the men involved, but in the sharp delineation of psychological attitudes toward winning and losing.

Minnesota Fats, played by Jackie Gleason, is a worthy champion. Here is this fat man, three hundred pounds from his embroidered satin coat down to his immaculate shoes, oozing grace and class, light as a cat on his feet around the table, utterly sure of himself in the game, a *winner*. He hasn't been beaten in fifteen years. And Eddie, bumpkin from Oakland, open-necked shirt and jeans, sweaty and unkempt. How can he possibly win? Well, tonight it's different.

On the stroke of eight o'clock, Minnesota Fats appears at the double doors. Strides in. Is divested of his jacket. Powders his hands. On the wall a laconic notice: "No Gambling." Turns to the new arrival.

" 'You like to gamble, Eddie? Gamble money on pool games?' " " 'Fats, let's you and I shoot a game of straight pool!' " " 'Hundred dollars?' " Eddie bumps it up to two hundred. " 'Now I know why they call you Fast Eddie. Eddie, you talk my kind of talk . . . rack 'em up!' " And there follows a fine and fluid scene of pool shooting, a long sequence of careening balls, cracking against one another like rifle shots, snapping into the pockets, rolling gently back to delicate angles, the faces of the two players absorbed, studied, appreciative of each other's artistry.

Eddie loses the first few games. The clock advances toward midnight. Everyone is watching the exhibition. Eddie is being cut up, and after each loss, Charlie's melancholic face appears as he hands over the lost stake.

Then the flow changes. Why? No apparent reason.

Fats misses one. " 'You don't leave much when you miss, do you, fat man?' " " 'That's what the game's all about.' " Eddie looks down, hits a tricky shot from a fine angle, and Fats compliments him. " 'I got a hunch, fat man, I got a hunch it's me from now on!' "

Eddie proceeds to take his opponent apart, winning game after game, smoothly, without a strain, like a finely tuned piece of machinery designed to sink balls around a pool table. Fats watches it all, a shade apprehensively, savoring Eddie's play despite himself. Eddie, in full flow, proposes raising the stakes to $1,000 a game. Fats assents, sends for whiskey, ice, and a glass; Eddie immediately calls for bourbon, no glass.

By dawn, Eddie is way ahead, his partner, Charlie, tells him—$18,000 cash—and Charlie wants to quit. Not Eddie. " 'The pool game is over when Fats says it's over.' " Charlie, small-town grafter, can't see it, Eddie hisses at him, that he came after Fats and now he's *got* him.

This is the crucial scene, the core of the movie, where it cruelly demonstrates the difference between winners and losers.

It turns on the intervention of another character who has made his appearance, drawn by the ripple of high action. He sits at the side of the pool table, a dark, hatchet-faced, sardonic-looking man, intent on the play, now and then exchanging glances with Minnesota Fats, calculating, missing nothing. He is the operator behind the scenes, the hustler who plays the other hustlers, the man who has a piece of the action in anything going. Though his name in the movie is Bert Gordon, no one could ever mistake him for anyone other than George C. Scott. Tonight he is backing Fats, despite Eddie's winning streak.

Fats shouts to keep the daylight out when someone raises the blinds. He goes to rinse his hands at a basin, washes his face and dusts his hands with powder. Eddie, meanwhile, is knocking back the last of the bourbon. " 'I'm gonna beat him, mister,' " Eddie confides to Bert Gordon, watching like a vulture to see where the pickings will fall. " 'I beat him all night and I'm gonna beat him all day.' " And to the freshly powdered Fats: " 'I'm the best you've ever seen, Fats, I'm the best there is. Even if you beat me, I'm still the best.'" Charlie is resigned, unhappily, to staying on in the saloon; he fears what's happening.

Gordon looks on, eyes narrowed. Then he delivers his verdict to Fats. "'Stay with this kid. *He's a loser.*'"

He knows, though it's not immediately apparent to the others in the saloon (or to us, the audience), that Eddie's a loser. Then Eddie, overwhelmed with his triumph, his inspired streak, starts falling about, giggling hysterically with the release of tension. He can't get over Fats's absurd appearance, all cleaned and laundered and powdered like a baby. He's beaten "the man." Oh, boy! Eddie shakes his head in amazed delight and disbelief, and he goes on playing . . .

The story cuts savagely to the next scene. Eddie has been busted. Beaten and broke, both; sprawled in a stupor as Fats racks up another game.

Exhausted as he is, he wants to go on with his last $200. Not Fats, though. He calls peremptorily for the stake money. "'The game's over, Eddie!'"

Eddie can't believe it, that Fats is going. "'You watch me!'" Fats says, pumping a wad of bank notes into Gordon's hand as he strides out.

For Eddie, stumbling down into the street with Charlie to find a fifth-rate hotel, it's all a might-have-been.

Why did Fats win? Obvious. He had the concentration of the winner. He paced himself, knew how to take his whiskey, how to handle himself through the night, how to wait out his opponent's streak, how to come back at dawn clean and clearheaded. There was no way Eddie could match an experienced competitor like Fats, even though for a spell he had the edge, his talent was supreme. That's not what winning is all about. It's control, money management, concentration. "'Everyone's got "talent,"'" Gordon tells him derisively.

A price has to be paid in becoming a winner, which helps

explain the curious thing about these gambling films: the relationship with women. It just never seems right. The Cincinnati Kid is involved with a sweet Southern girl called Christian, all sighs and corn-colored hair and innocence; and although this down-home girl (Tuesday Weld) is recognizable as a type, there seems no rhyme or reason why the Kid should be so enamored of her. Maybe he's just a simple down-home boy himself at heart, but if so, what's he doing on the big-time gambling scene? The screenwriters gave the story a further dimension, not in the book, by bringing in a real flesh-and-blood woman, no better than she should be (Ann-Margret), to make a pass at the Kid. But this would-be passionate interlude seems no more than a thin device for filling in time in the movie, before we get to the showdown over the card table.

The romantic angle is even more strained in *The Hustler*. Fast Eddie meets a lady in distress who has turned to the bottle because of some kind of deep blues regarding her love life, and they move in together.

Their amorous attachment might be believable if the girl came across with some style or conviction, but with Piper Laurie playing her as a fading high-school queen, it never catches fire. Her drinking problem turns to morning coffee; her show of passion is confined to a glimpse of her slip.

Winners don't have time for girls, it seems. As Lancey puts it to the Kid, " 'Women are a universal problem in our game.' " He advises against permanent attachments. A winning player's entire life is dedicated to the mastery of winning. In *The Hustler*, it is Bert Gordon, the operator, who inculcates the lesson in Eddie.

Gordon sets Eddie up in a private match against a rich old amateur who fancies his chances at billiards. But there's a surprise when they set off to meet him: Eddie shows up with his girl. She, with her nebulous possessiveness, gets on the wrong side of Gordon right away, and he starts trying to humiliate her. It's not an unmotivated nastiness. Gordon knows that Eddie won't be a winner while he's distracted by her presence.

Down in the billiard room the winning and losing themes of *The Hustler* come together. Because Eddie still hasn't got the killer instinct, he starts losing, and Gordon refuses to go on staking him. Eddie is incensed; he knows he can take this plummy old boy.

Meanwhile, Eddie's girl has gotten drunk—feeling sorry for herself, which Gordon says is the occupational excuse of losers—and late at night she stumbles downstairs, interrupting the game. Eddie is annoyed by her presence, tries to be patient, loses his temper, and slings her out—the precise point at which Gordon comes in with the money. He sees that Eddie means to win and win big. Not just that he *can* win but that he *will* win. Which he does in short order.

So a new, hardened Fast Eddie goes back to Ames's saloon and challenges Fats again. This time he whips him and whips him good. Fats, the master, is dethroned, but Eddie's victory is hollow. A winner himself, he loses the girl (who dies from an overdose).

By contrast, the Cincinnati Kid, a loser, goes back to his girl (so the original story has it; the movie doesn't say).

Neither denouement really works. The Kid isn't a loser; his first love will always be the game; and it's obvious enough that he will be back there, however he makes it up with his girl. As for Eddie, his conclusion is not at all borne out by what has gone before: "'I loved her, but I traded her in for a pool game.'" This is not justified, either by the story itself, nor, more importantly, by the feelings which Eddie has demonstrated.

The Hustler poses the right question in the conflict between private life and public winning, which psychologically lies at the heart of all competitive games. But the answer it gives, in implying that the one can only be fulfilled by elimination of the other, is too stark. Nevertheless, producer and director

Robert Rossen's film is probably the definitive statement about winning and losing in games, if not in life. Although *The Hustler* is about pool, its lessons apply just as strongly, indeed precisely, to poker.

CHAPTER EIGHT

The Old, Old Story

First get your man, then get your hand.
—ERIC STEINER

Tonight's the night!

From the very first ring of the alarm, in all the bedrooms across the suburbs, the day feels entirely different. Through our humdrum lives a little snake of excitement goes licking and darting its way, the tingle of anticipation. Why is tonight different from all the other nights? Yes . . . but in another sense, it's the same the world over.

Although the characters in this little drama are fictitious, including the narrator, you can recognize them, more or less, from any poker game you've ever sat in.

Breakfasttime . . .

"You're not playing again tonight, Dave darling?"

"Uh-huh."

"But you know we're supposed to be going to my mother's."

"But it's *Tues*day, Agnes."

"Do you always have to play every Tuesday? We haven't been out for weeks!"

"Can't we go to your mother's tomorrow night? I'd love to go to your mother's. Any night but tonight. You see, the guys are de*pend*ing on me. I just can't let them down."

"So what time are you going out?"

"Um, well, actually the game's *here* tonight. Could you rustle up some snacks or salad or something? I mean, please don't go to any trouble . . ."

The office phone . . .

"Can I speak to Melvin? Sure, it's important! Well, interrupt him, please. . . . Melvin, how are you fixed tonight? Yes, we've got four, but we've got to find one more, *min*imum. What do you mean, your sister from Australia? You must be kidding! Melvin, this is important, we *need* you. Yes, I know, I feel lousy too. I'll give you some aspirin. Of course we're quitting early! Listen, I can't go on after midnight, say twelve-thirty absolute limit. I've got a mountain of work here—Hold on a minute, Melvin. . . . Yes, Mr. Schneider. No, Mr. Schneider. I'll be right with you, sir. I must just clear this call with the downtown office. . . . Melvin? Listen, what are you doing, keeping me all morning on the telephone? You're ruining my career. Just *be* there."

"Hello, Tom? I'm doubtful about Melvin. You think he means it? I'm going to call his home later just to make sure. Listen, that's not the big problem. I'm worried about Harry. Do you think he can *afford* it? I mean he lost a hundred and fifty last week and two hundred and fifty the week before. . . . What do you mean? We all play badly, for Christ's sake. Everyone except you. It's not a matter of playing badly; it's a matter of whether his check goes through. Look, I've busted my ass organizing this goddamn game, and now you tell me I'm responsible for Harry. I've been losing too. Yeah, well maybe I did. I was just lucky, that's all. You mean if there's any trouble with the check we can work it out later? Sure, sure, it may never happen."

"Hello, Cora, is Harry there? Why, no, Cora, I just wondered if—um—Harry was doing anything tonight. . . . No indeed, not in the least. Thank you very much, Cora. Harry? Yes, we're playing at my place tonight. Listen, Harry, I'm worried about . . . Do you think the stakes are too *high?*

Well, you know, one week you lose and one week I lose, and maybe we should reduce the ante or something? Okay, okay, don't shout. I agree with you. You can't run a bluff without a big bet at the end. Listen, Harry, that check of yours, can I put it in now? The end of the month? Fine, Harry, just fine."

"Is Melvin in? Meeting his sister? Please take a message for him. . . . Just remind him that the conference will be at nine o'clock tonight, and we're expecting him. Would you say that it is very important indeed that he arrives on time?"

Meanwhile back at the ranch . . .

"Mother, Dave's tied up at the office tonight. He's so sorry. There's very little chance, he says, but he'll try. That Mr. Schneider drives him like a slave. Why, no, Mother, they think very highly of him at the office. He's so conscientious."

"Hi there, Agnes!"

"Hi, Agnes, honey, you're looking great. Say, am I the first?"

"Hi, honey, you're looking marvelous. Say, where's the ice?"

"Hi, honey, you're looking terrific. Hey, Tom, you know that hand of seven card last week when you had the high flush? I just realized how I should've played it. You remember the last card, what happened was . . ."

"Listen, Melvin, just to get things moving, will you loosen up tonight?"

"Listen to Dave, the tightest player in the game!"

"Wha'd'ya mean? I'm the tightest player in the country!"

"The way Tom hits cards he doesn't need to bluff."

"I tried a bluff last year, didn't work."

"Hey, have you seen the new girl in Harry's office?"

"I bought five hundred Electronic Comestibles last week. Know anything about 'em?"

"Listen! Hold it! Can I ask a simple question? CAN I ASK A SIMPLE QUESTION? Did we come here to have a social conversation or did we come here to play poker?"

Overgrown schoolboys. Are we all rather ridiculous? Or are we just nervous before the action, weekend paratroopers waiting to jump? Right from the first hand, anyway, the jokes fall away, a sudden quiet descends over the room.

This game is dealer's choice. As usually happens, a couple of fellows have shown up at the last minute because they couldn't bear to stay away, and we have a full table. Everyone counts out 500 in chips, blue hundreds, red fifties, pink twenty-fives, and a mound of white ones for the smaller units. Melvin, who is very cautious, squirrels 250 in his pocket. We don't cut for seats and there is a bit of jockeying by everyone to get his favorite place. It's a round table, so what difference does it make? Answer: Could be. I move in to the left of Tom, a fire raiser and the most dangerous player in the game, because sitting immediately over him enables me to fold cheaply when he plays fast and loose. He knows what I'm up to, but as I am overtight in my pattern of play, he sees no threat in having me there; if I do come in after one of his wild reraises, he knows I've got something. On my other side is Dick, an amusing, chatty kind of player, who always insists on showing you his hole cards when you're out of a hand; by sitting left of me and of Tom, Dick thinks he has double protection. What he doesn't know is that every time he's planning a raise, he gives it away in advance by dipping in his bin to count out the chips.

First choice is seven card hi-lo, which goes a complete round of the table before the next man's choice. The cards are shuffled; the mysterious tensions coiled and hidden in their random weaving are about to be released. I fold a medium-looking card. "There goes Dave!" someone quips, and the next up card falls with a crisp little *snap!* around the table in front of each player. All but two players drop and the pot is split without a contest. This is early in the evening; the play is just flexing up. "If you don't win the first pot, you can't win 'em all." I fold again. Plenty of time, plenty of hands to come. We shall all sit next to one another, linked by the invisible bonds of poker, for six or seven hours tonight, or even longer. How long can you sit in a theater? How long do you stay with your hosts at a dinner party? And we have done this week after week for months and years. We know one another, in some ways, better than our wives and mothers do. It's a strange relationship of warmth and contest.

Finally I get involved in a hand. This is a wild variation we play, which I usually avoid because it's so chancy and hard to read: five card hi-lo with the hair-raising peculiarity that if you pair any up card with your hole card they're both jokers, plus a twist at the end. Zowie!

Sitting on four medium kind of cards to the queen, with nothing much showing against me, I decide to go with this hand as if the queen had just paired one in the hole, meaning they were both wild.

"Raise!" I announce suddenly.

"Uh-huh, Dave's hit one at last!" someone warns. I give an embarrassed little smile because that's the story I want them to believe. Two players call, two problems. First comes Melvin, who is showing lower cards; okay, he probably started with a pair in the hole, and is drawing to an unbeatable low.

The second problem is Harry, who has been seduced by a pair of nines showing, but without a paired card in the hole to back them with—which would give him four of a kind—is merely hanging on, hoping to match his hole card, whatever it is. So what is it? He *can't* have a nine down there, which would give him three wild cards, because one has already gone and I've caught the case nine. Last up card and Harry bets weakly. So I wade in by raising the pot again. Melvin calls and Harry (who is a successful fake-antique dealer but a lousy card player) also just calls. If he'd reraised, I would have *had* to believe he'd paired in the hole to give him four nines.

So that leaves the two of them still. Melvin didn't reraise, but I have a nasty feeling he knows I'm trying to pull something. Okay, let's see how strong he is. It doesn't worry me that he will be drawing to a lower hand than mine on the final twist, because I'm counting on Harry to drop. Then with just two of us left in I can wriggle out simply by going the opposite way to Melvin on the declaration.

Harry	(?)	9 ♥ 9 ♣ A ♣	~~J ♣~~ / 10 ♠	
Dave	(4 ♠)	2 ♥ Q ♠	~~9 ♦~~ / J ♠	7 ♣
Melvin	(?)	3 ♠ 5 ♥ 7 ♦	~~8 ♠~~ / 2 ♦	

Trouble! I throw away my next highest card, as I would naturally do if my queens were paired, and I catch a J ♠—no help. But Melvin gets a nice little deuce for his eight.

Harry checks. Still no pair in the hole for wild cards; he isn't that subtle to check a cinch if he had one. So I bet half the pot, to reinforce Melvin's impression that my queens really are paired and to drive Harry out. He peeks long and disgustedly at his hole card before folding.

So far so good. Now for Melvin. His low is solid, but surely he must believe my queens are paired, giving me three jacks for high. I bet strongly when the queen hit and am marked for higher trips than his trips with a three in the hole. My final bet has made it too expensive for him to take a chance, or was that the error? Because with hardly a pause or hesitation he comes up with two coins in his hand for both ways. I'm cooked.

Throwing away my cards before anyone can analyze my feeble bluff, I ask Melvin how he knew what I was up to. "Your ears waggled," he tells me.

I make a mental note to avoid that play, for now I recall that he caught me on a similar coup a couple of weeks back, which, just possibly, he remembered now. All right, Melvin, watch out. Next time around I'll be loaded! Meanwhile, I've lost nearly half my chips in the first hour's play. Making the most of my misfortune by loudly demanding a second stack, I complain that they're taking me to the cleaners.

Then I make a bad play, perhaps induced by the previous miscalculation. This time it's five card hi-lo draw, which is a tricky game requiring plenty of nerve. There is no way you can be sure when it comes to declaring at the end which way the other man's going. Drawing one card, the odds are he's going for a low hand, but he may also be trying to hit two pairs or a flush.

Sitting under the gun, I pick up A-2-4-6-7, a terrific hand. Too good to open in this position, so I check. It's opened on my other side by Dick; Tom calls. Back to me and I wade in with the maximum raise. They both call, without enthusiasm. The phone starts ringing but I don't let it distract me. On the draw I stand pat, of course, and bet the pot. I want them to fold, rather than one player, assuming I'm low, backing in for the high half of the pot on just a pair.

Dick, on a one card draw, folds. "I've probably got it both ways, but I'm gonna let you take it," he announces. He's a better player than he sounds, but he obviously missed his low. Tom, who bought two cards, comes back from the phone, looks at his draw briefly, and all in the same gesture raises the whole pot back—75 in chips goes hurtling in—with a typically careless flourish.

Now what does that mean? Tom knows that its odds-on I'm

going for the low with my hand—low hands are frequently dealt pat, highs much more rarely. And he knows I know he knows, if you follow me. So he could simply be trying to frighten me out if I have only a moderate low, because he's convinced, if I do call, that his hand will stand up for high in any case. I look at him sitting next to me, calmly puffing a cigarette, squinting slightly in the smoke, giving nothing away whatever. This is just the kind of aggressive opportunism he excels at.

Did he have trips before the draw? He didn't raise on them, but the same argument holds for a pair and a kicker.

Alternatively, having bought two cards, can he really be low? He does try that sometimes, but the odds are enormous that he can outdraw me, with a 7-6.

I hover. I think he *must* have made a fantastic buy for low. But if I fold this one, he's going to have a psychological edge over me in every hand for the rest of the night. I haven't got the inspiration to go high or the resolution to fold. I push my chips in and call low.

Tom spreads a cold 6-4 at me. "Tough luck!" He grins. "Nice draw," I answer evenly. "Keep trying it."

Tom is an ad man, by profession as well as in poker, and the way he mixes it at hi-lo when he's on form is so damn demoralizing I have to admire it in spite of myself. In fact, over recent weeks he has, as chess players would term it, a plus score against me. Can he really be not just a better player but *that* much better? I grind out the end of a cigar. "Let's have a light, you lucky sonofabitch!"

Midnight and down two stacks. No cards, no chances. The game is really rolling now; each hand is being contested well. I've split a couple of miserable pots, but can't make any impression on the game. Then at last I get into a hand, a big one. It's seven card hi-lo and I find (A ♠ 2 ♦) 6 ♠.

It's opened, I call, and Tom, showing a 3 ♣, raises. No need to push at this point, so I call. Next card for me is pretty useful, a 7 ♦. With four cards for a strong low, I am odds-on and will have to see this one through all the way.

Tom is also showing two low cards, but mine are better; the only other interesting hand around is Melvin's, with a pair of sevens, which could be going either way.

It's checked around to me, I bet the pot, and still they all call. Then I start to go wrong, with a queen. It's still good odds for me to hit the low, so I raise regardless, and the pair of sevens raises me back. Why? I don't believe it's trips; he's trying to semibluff that he *has* got trips.

Tom calls, clearly going for low, and two other players also call. Sixth card gives me another useless queen, which practically ruins me.

Dave	(A ♠ 2 ♦) 6 ♠ 7 ♦ Q ♠ Q ♦
Melvin	(? ?) 7 ♥ 7 ♣ 2 ♣ K ♠
Tom	(? ?) 3 ♣ 8 ♠ 10 ♥ 5 ♥

I bet the pair of queens showing, in the vague hope that one of the others may drop. Melvin calls. He could be going either way, but with trips, surely he'd bet again. Tom raises. What he's got this time? He could be drawing to an eight low or even a six low. I don't think he can really be trying for high, when both the other hands have pairs showing. I could reraise to try to blast out Melvin, but having come so far, I think he'll stay. So I call, without pausing, and Melvin follows. I await the final card with trepidation, and peeping at it in the hole, I find the worst: a lousy, stinking K ♥. No high, no low, squeezed like a lemon.

I look around the board, wondering desperately how I'm going to get out of this one. There's more than 200 in the pot and this looks like the make-or-break hand. I can't afford to check, because any sign of weakness will finish me. But if I

make a heavy bet, the boys will still read me as weak and suspect I'm trying to buy the pot. Somehow I've got to provoke
the opportunity to reraise and show strength that way.

"Let's try a little pink 'un." Trying to sound casual, I toss in
a large pink 25 chip, a "feeler" bet. It falls on the pile in the
middle with an ominous plink.

Melvin, on his two sevens, looks a shade unhappy, but he's
in too deep to pull out now. He just calls, which suggests he's
not overly strong. As I hoped he would, Tom now raises half
the pot with his usual abandon. I'm convinced Tom has caught
a low on the last card and his raise gives me the chance to
crack the whip hard by sticking all my remaining chips in. If
Melvin folds, as he damned well ought to do, I can salvage
half the pot for high. He thinks a while, fingering his chips,
and finally calls. "Poppa's comin' a-l-l the way this time," he
croons, but he's biting his lower lip, a nervous way he has.

The problem for me is whether Melvin really has his two
pairs. My final king is one he hasn't got, and another has
shown; my seven still leaves the fourth somewhere. His two is
not a problem because he surely won't go high with sevens up.

I show one coin in my hand for high. My gut is puckering
as I look around. But relief surges over me as I see both the
others have called low. Tom has a 10-8 against Melvin's 10-7.

None of us should have gone so far, but we'd all gotten "involved." In fact, Tom had two little pairs, fives and threes, and
was trying to sneak up on us—looking deceptively low all the
way—by hitting a hidden full house. As it turned out, if he'd
stayed with his two little pairs they would have beaten my
queens.

"What did you have for high?" he inquires.

"Oh, I was loaded that time," I tell him, spreading the hand.

"Wha'd'ya mean?" protests Harry, watching from the side-
lines. "You just had a lousy pair of queens!"

"Is that so?" I exclaim with mock innocence. "I thought I

caught my flush! What were you for high, Tom?" I ask sweetly, as Melvin divides the pot. But Tom, frowning, has buried his winning two pairs in the discards. He is still way ahead but the flow has changed.

In the ideal poker game, I suppose one would start winning, go on winning pot after pot, and keep on winning right up to the last hand of the night. But somehow, for reasons that I've never quite explained to myself, psychologically I find it most satisfying when I start losing, get into deep trouble, fight my way back, and just in the last hour come charging out ahead. Maybe this is one of those nights.

It's one o'clock and the feeling of having come back from three stacks down to almost level is intoxicating. Time to change the pace! I start to get aggressive, raising on the first card, pushing my confidence, cutting a swath through the hands, and am rewarded with several small pots. I get my own back against Melvin, at five card stud, by raising him with just a pair of aces, when he had already bet on an open pair.

"I could have had you beat!" he protests. "I'm surprised you went against the percentages."

"Oh, well, Melvin, I came here to gamble!"

"That'll be the day," someone else growls.

I grab a sandwich in the kitchen, gulp down a can of beer (drinking at poker is a mistake, but this calls for a celebration), and yell through the door to deal me in the hand.

"Hey, how long are we going on?" someone inquires. "Two o'clock?"

"Naw, for Chrissake," one of the losers complains, "three o'clock's our regular time."

"How about a last round at two-thirty?" someone suggests.

"It's all right for you guys," I complain. "Some of us have a job to hold down." Ribald laughter.

"Deal, dammit, deal!"

Then one of those squalls blows up. On an innocuous hand of seven card hi-lo, Melvin raises out of turn, or rather, not out of turn, but just as Harry, sitting in front of him, was about to sling his chips into the pot.

"If you're raising, I don't call," says Harry, pulling his money back.

"What d'ya mean, you don't call? You already called the bet!"

"My money wasn't in the pot. You bet out of turn! Didn't he?" Harry swings around for support.

"Look, what is this?" bawls Melvin, who has a short temper. "Is this a serious poker game or are we making up the rules as we go along?"

"Speak for yourself!"

Suddenly everyone is shouting and arguing across the table; the place is bedlam. The noise comes to an abrupt stop as Melvin, glasses down his nose, hair awry, pushes his chair back and lumbers to his feet.

"All right! If that's the way you want to play, play by yourselves. I'm quitting!" He zips up his Windbreaker. "And don't expect to see me again. This is the last time I ever play here."

"Now wait a moment, Melvin . . ."

"Hold it . . ."

"Will ya listen to me . . ."

"If the money's so goddamn important . . ."

"You didn't see what happened . . ."

"Damn right I saw what happened . . ."

"What kind of a game is this?"

Everyone has his own suggestion to put things right. During the argument, Melvin sits down aggrievedly. It takes ten minutes to assuage angry feelings and restore order. Then we change around flats.

"Who dealt this mess?"

"What are we playing anyway?"

"Awright, deal!"

In a forced silence, the game starts up again.

Two o'clock, I'm ahead and overconfident and come a crop-
per. I'm dealt (10-10)-K at seven card high, a goodish hand
but needs protection. I raise, and they all fold except Dick.
My next card is an ace. That looks strong, and as my opening
raise gave me the initiative, I bet again. Dick calls it. He's a
steady kind of player, as you'd expect a doctor to be, and behind a string of facetious chatter, he's basically quite careful.

What's gotten into him? He's showing just two medium
cards, off suit. "There are only four aces in the deck," I tell
him, fishing. "What can you possibly have?"

"Oh, are there only four aces?" he ripostes, grinning. "I
thought I'd keep a spare one up my sleeve."

My next card is a blank, but Dick's doesn't help him either.
I check to see what he does, and he checks too. My sixth card
again is no help, but Dick gets an ace, which makes my hand
look that much less strong, despite my overlay. We both check
along.

Last card in the hole—hooray!—is a ten, giving me trips.
I've got him nailed. "Well, I don't know, doctor," I observe,
sounding like a consultant giving a second opinion, "I'll raise
the pot while you count the aces again." I want him to think
I'm bluffing on two pairs if he's got aces up. He's suddenly become very silent, which is usually a telltale sign of strength.
To my surprise, Dick raises back the pot, and to my consterna-
tion I suddenly notice that the ace and the first up card in his
hand are both hearts. It didn't register before.

| Dave | (10 ♥ 10 ♠) K ♦ A ♠ 3 ♣ 8 ♣ (10 ♣) |
| Dick | (?   ?) J ♥ 6 ♦ 7 ♣ A ♥ (?) |

Can Dick have stayed in for my opening raises on two high
hearts? At this stage I'm too befuddled to recall how many

hearts have fallen. I should never have checked on the sixth card. On the other hand, there's a lot of money in the pot . . . I call, and Dick flips over his hole cards, the king and two low hearts.

"Doctor"—I smile bravely—"do you carry tranquilizers with you?" That earns a laugh but leaves me feeling deflated and angry with myself. I'm no longer ahead.

Two-thirty, everyone's tired, the game is slower. Tom is sitting on his winnings and has stopped raising so wildly. I douse my face under the cold tap. In the yellow arc of light from the door, the boys are slouched around the table in a haze of smoke and sweat and whiskey. Surely, I can finally get a grip on this session.

"What time do you serve breakfast in this joint?" someone demands.

"You got the money, honey, I got the time."

Up to now, I've had to work at my hands, but here comes an easy ride. At least that's how it looked to start with. It's five card stud hi-lo with a twist, a game where the last card makes or breaks your hand without fear or favor.

I start with (2 ♣) 3 ♦ and then catch a 4 ♥. Terrific potential for either way, so I raise. There are some good hands showing around the table, but if my next card is low, I'm going to be very strong. No one will be able to read which way I'm going (I won't even know myself). Three players call and I catch a 6 ♠.

Dave	(2 ♣) 3 ♦ 4 ♥ 6 ♠
Harry	(?) 7 ♦ 8 ♥ A ♣
Tom	(?) 10 ♥ 4 ♠ 10 ♣
Dick	(?) 8 ♣ 8 ♦ 9 ♥

The board shows Dick and Tom going for high, with open pairs showing—and they must be feeling a bit uneasy with my possible straight building—and Harry challenging me for low. But he is showing not just one card worse than mine, but two. If he throws the eight on the change, he will still be drawing to a worse hand than mine. No problem there.

So when Tom, as high man, bets his pair of tens, I pour it on. Everyone calls; it's late and the losers are pushing their luck too hard to drop now. Fifth card is another six, not what I wanted, but Harry gets a ten. I'm still strong, with chances to hit a cinch low and a straight as well if I pull the magic five. I deliberate whether to raise again and decide just to call. It can go wrong, after all. Now we change cards. Harry throws his ten and I throw my second six. But whereas he catches the five I wanted in order to lift the whole pot, I'm ruined with a queen!

| Dave | (2 ♣) 3 ♦ 4 ♥ 6 ♠ ~~6 ♣~~ Q ♦ |
| Harry | (?) 7 ♦ 8 ♥ A ♣ ~~10 ♦~~ 5 ♠ |

The high hands don't bother me, of course, because they're both showing open pairs. Tom bets lightly on his tens. He could have trips, more likely just the pair. Dick just calls. Maybe he hasn't got trips, but he can certainly beat tens. What am I to do now?

Harry's going to raise after me whether he's got it or not. It's an absolutely classical position: he can squeeze me till the pits squeak. I gaze at his hand: (?)-7-8-A-5, sitting after my beautiful (2)-3-4-6-lousy queen. Is there any way Harry could go wrong?

"How much money have you got there, Harry?" I inquire, playing for time. "Oh, about two hundred," he says brightly.

That is going to be the price of my seeing this one through if I stick it in. A loser for the night, a sorehead for the week, *if* he's got it.

To try to convince myself, I start reading the possibilities out loud. "You threw a ten and caught a five. The five didn't pair you, did it, Harry? There's one gone and Dick's got one showing. Now you haven't got eights, have you, Harry? [I don't bother to speculate about the ace, because if Harry is paired on aces, he'll be in the hand for the high, anyway.] Did you pair the sevens? Haven't seen any sevens around."

Harry is sitting quite still, trying to look enigmatic. Finally he opens his mouth. "Why don't you either crap or get off the pot!"

I just can't make up my mind about the sevens. Harry is a bad enough player to stick around with a low pair wired, hoping to surprise the other high hands with a second pair; on the other hand, at this stage of the night, he could well have bucked the odds to outdraw me for low. I hate to see a pot like this slip away . . .

"All right, Harry," I tell him resolutely, "you're a nice feller." And I shove the money in for the call.

Harry perks up, seizes the rest of his chips with both hands in a flamboyant flourish and announces "Raise!"

He's got me! I think immediately. But here's one of those funny things: Harry's counting out of his chips is a mite over deliberate. There's some sort of high-frequency wave that his gesture transmits which tells me—one can't quite define it; it comes from playing with the same personalities month in and month out, a sense that maybe he's just making too much of counting his chips out—which tells me all is not right with Harry's hand.

Now the betting is back to the high hands. Tom, with just a pair, folds. He's well ahead of the game and is afraid of Dick's eights (which are, in fact, trips). Maybe I ought not to call Harry's raise, but having started out on this thing, I have to see it through now. Our fists all dive down beneath the table, juggling with the coins to make the final declaration. Up we come. Naturally, Harry's called low.

"Are you paired?" I inquire mildly, with a dry mouth.

"No," says Harry. And he turns his hole card. A big, fat king is sitting there! Well, we-e-ll, well . . .

"You see, I *had* to bet it that way," Harry says, justifying his play. "That was the only way to do it, because . . ."

"Sure," I tell him, raking in my half of the pot, a mound of chips, "you played it exactly right, Harry."

"Is this the last round?"

"What d'ya mean? Frightened of losing your winnings?"

"Three-thirty and then quit, right?"

"How about a final round of seven card hi-lo, just to finish it off?"

"Let's have one round of seven hi-lo and one of dealers!"

"Look, I have a helluva day tomorrow . . ."

"Four o'clock, final!"

"Absolute deadline!"

"No last round, no last hand, just stop then, right?"

"Four o'clock and then *quit*, and I mean *quit*."

It's turned four o'clock. This is the last round, the late-night final extra. Tom is well ahead; I'm not so far behind him. Harry's come back to about level for a change and is elated at his "success." Dick and Melvin and the others are paying for the party. We add up the chips, additions and subtractions are calculated, checks—at last—are written. Someone draws the curtain and a pink-gray dawn races over the room, obliterating the stale light like a cloth rubbed over an old slate.

"Oh, no-o-o!"

"It's too late to hit the sack now, baby!"

"Let's shoot downtown for some breakfast!"

"C'mon, let's go!"

As the boys pile out the door someone calls over his shoulder, "Hey, where's it at next week?"

CHAPTER NINE

Funny Deal

Your first duty is to the Game; then come Mother, God, and Country.
—Old saying at the National Press Club, Washington, D.C.

Ricky showed up one night at our game via a telephone call from a friend of a friend. If we had a seat open, he said boyishly—he was a fresh-faced, neatly dressed fellow in his early thirties, with curly brown hair and a mother's boy smile—then he would be delighted to pitch in. A new player is always welcome, right? What with guys being out of town or struck down with flu or involved in family reunions with a long-lost uncle from Oshkosh, or simply being busted out of the game, a new man is doubly welcome. Even better, Ricky was the son of an oil millionaire or something like that, and he exuded a certain air of prosperity in his pin-stripe shirt and gold cuff links. At the very least, it was clear that he was not worried about where his next meal was coming from, and we dealt him in.

At the table, Ricky's deportment was ideal: alert, polite, a good winner, and on this occasion a good loser. He played well but not too well and, a most engaging quality, he obviously adored poker. He was not one to quit at 2 or 3 A.M., or when the last round was finally, reluctantly, agreed upon by the losers, at 3:30 A.M. He was on for the night and the next day too. With rueful grace he wrote out his check—at something over $600, it was a heavy loss in this game—and turning to another loser who had been desperately trying to prolong the game, he proposed a final half-hour of two-handed. If he was on, Ricky was on. My obligations as host being over, I wished them *bonne chance* and hit the sack.

191

Coming down to breakfast some hours later, I found the lights still on. Ricky seemed just as debonair as when he had walked in the night before. His opponent looked as soggy as a milk pudding. There was a big pile of chips in front of Ricky. "My God," cried the other fellow in a memorable phrase, "this guy plays worse than anyone I have ever played with since I was at school, and he's winning all my money!"

Ricky smiled agreeably through the haze of smoke as the curtains let in the daylight. "Your deal, I think?"

The same pattern was repeated two or three times more. Ricky lost, playing a sporting but quite accurate game in the main session, and then went on to clean up anyone who showed the temerity to take him on at cutthroat. The morning after one such game, I got a frantic telephone call. It was from Al, one of the best players in our group. He had not gone to bed yet and was in a state of dazed excitement. The burden of his message was that he had dropped nearly a thousand. "This guy Ricky is incredible! Some of the calls he makes, there's just *no way* he can do it!"

What particularly struck my friend was that at five card stud hi-lo, with a change of card at the end, a game much favored by us because of its fast action and opportunities in going "the wrong way" in declaring at the end, Ricky kept burning him. He made calls for which there was no possible justification, and each time won the hand.

For instance, if Al discarded a queen to go for low, catching a jack instead, making (?)-2-3-7-$\frac{Q}{J}$ against (?)-5-8-9-$\frac{3}{K}$, the king having replaced a three, Al has to all intents and purposes a cinch low. Obviously Ricky's discard of the three implies that he has a low card in the hole, probably a six or a seven, giving him a chance of a straight for hi-lo; but when he catches a king against a jack showing, he can't be lower and has no choice but to go high against it. Al can't win anything in a split pot, but it is hardly conceivable that he can lose his half of the pot. He would bet his low hand, Ricky would raise, and Al would call. And in the declaration, done simultaneously with a coin in the hand, Ricky would call *low* on his king. Al, despite being marked low all the way along, would lose.

$$(3) \ 2\ 3\ 7\ J$$
$$(6) \ 5\ 8\ 9\ K$$

"How the hell could you call low on your king?" he would demand incredulously.

Ricky would smile his pleasant boyish smile. "Oh, I just had a feeling, you know, from the way you didn't reraise at the end that you were paired up. Your deal, I think?"

Or the other way around: Ricky would raise into possible straights or high pairs and then call high, winning on deuces wired. "I just had a hunch you hadn't got the pair, you know." Of course Ricky could somehow "psych" out his opponent's weak hole card and call high, but there was no way he could *bet* into such hands.

Here's a really flagrant example of play against the run of the cards. Al is showing (?)-8-7-6-5 and betting hard all the way against (?)-K-Q-3-9. Naturally, on the change he draws a card in the hole, with excellent chances of a straight, which will give him a lock high and low, and overwhelming chances of a cinch low, with an A, 2, 3, 4, 9, 10, J, Q, K winning for him. Ricky, who really has no business being in the pot at all, except that with a pair of kings or queens he has chances of saving his money on the high call, stands pat. And then he bets. Al has drawn an eight, which is a bad card, but there is still no justification for Ricky to call low, so Al reraises just to establish his strength for the low. And Ricky, with no pair, but (A)-K-Q-3-9 also goes low against (8)-8-7-6-5 and wins a huge pot.

Al was going out of his mind. Everyone knows, of course,

that cheats are drawn to cards like maggots to blue cheese and that there is just no way of getting away from them. But this was a private, friendly game, in which everyone else had known one another for quite a long while. Although Ricky was a new member in the game, he was not only a sporting player and amusing company, he was, on balance, barely a winner. He kept losing in the full game and kept getting it back at cutthroat. Can you accuse that sort of man, with that sort of track record, in this sort of group, of cheating? The consensus was No. Besides, there was no proof. He just kept making these incredible calls. It became something of a fascination to Al, and he went on playing Ricky two-handed, taking the precaution of avoiding a five-card game where the identity of a single hole card was crucial, and sticking to seven card hi-lo. And since Ricky played and lost so regularly in the main game, it seemed that even if there was something funny going on at two-handed, it was all right in the big game where everyone shuffled in turn and Ricky dealt only once out of seven times. Not an ideal situation, but there it was.

So one night the game moved to Ricky's place. The girl friend is making coffee, a bottle of Scotch is on the sideboard, everything is just as it should be. It so happened there were only five players this night: Ricky, three of the regular group, and a pal of his, an older fellow called (let us say) Paddy O'Fixit. Someone else showed up at the door later on, apparently wanting to play, but Ricky told his girl to send him away because they didn't need another player. The game rocks on and around midnight up comes the following hand at seven card hi-lo. The first bet is only 25¢, but before this hand is through there will be almost $8,500 on the table.

Paddy deals:

A	(J ♠ J ♦) J ♥
B	(A ♠ 5 ♣) 3 ♦

C	(Q ♥ Q ♣) 2 ♥
Ricky	(? ?) 4 ♥
Paddy	(? ?) 10 ♠

A bets the opening 25¢; B and C call; Ricky raises the limit (half the pot, which means all of 50¢ at this stage); Paddy calls; and the others merely come in. In the pot, a grand total of $4.50.

Next card shows:

A	(J ♠ J ♦) J ♥ 4 ♦
B	(A ♠ 5 ♣) 3 ♦ 4 ♣
C	(Q ♥ Q ♣) 2 ♥ Q ♦
Ricky	(? ?) 4 ♥ A ♣
Paddy	(? ?) 10 ♠ 9 ♠

Ricky, as high man, bets half the pot; Paddy calls; A raises; B, snake in the grass, merely calls; C reraises; Ricky reraises $10. A, not wanting to scare the fish, calls the reraise and everyone else comes in. In the pot, $90.

On the fifth card, there is some real action. A's three jacks still look good; B draws a seven low; C, with his three queens, catches an ace, which disguises his hand to make it look as if he may be going for low; Ricky gets the 8 ♥, which is a useful-looking low but not as strong as B's; and Paddy catches a third spade showing, the 6 ♠.

A	(J ♠ J ♦) J ♥ 4 ♦ 8 ♦
B	(A ♠ 5 ♣) 3 ♦ 4 ♣ 7 ♣
C	(Q ♥ Q ♣) 2 ♥ Q ♦ A ♥
Ricky	(? ?) 4 ♥ A ♣ 8 ♥
Paddy	(? ?) 10 ♠ 9 ♠ 6 ♠

It's obvious that this is going to be one hell of a hand because everyone looks loaded. C, with his ace-queen showing, bets half the pot; it goes around to A, who has no worry with his trips, and calls; B, now that his seven low is made, raises. Next thing, Paddy, showing 10 ♠ 9 ♠ 6 ♠, makes a huge reraise, $200. This is a surprising bet because he has up to now shown himself to be a very conservative player, folding early, betting tightly, and taking no risks. This reraise is way out of character. He can't possibly have a straight flush, can he? Straight flushes just don't happen at poker. Still, everyone is fairly leary of him because they haven't played with him before and don't know his style, so they just call the bet, thinking it may be some misguided semibluff. In the pot, a grand total of $1,460, starting from the dealer's original ante of 50¢.

But the point about this hand all the way through is that the way the cards fell, everyone *had* to be in.

Then on the sixth card an even more surprising thing happens. Having raised the pot with his huge bet, Paddy quietly turns over his cards and folds the next bet, which is a "feeler" from C, who has hit his full house queens. Meanwhile, B has caught a six for a six-five low, and seeing that no one is lower than he on the table, he raises back a testing $500.

A	(J ♠ J ♦) J ♥ 4 ♦ 8 ♦ 2 ♦	
B	(A ♠ 5 ♣) 3 ♦ 4 ♣ 7 ♣ 6 ♦	
C	(Q ♥ Q ♣) 2 ♥ Q ♦ A ♥ 2 ♣	
Ricky	(? ?) 4 ♥ A ♣ 8 ♥ 7 ♥	

C is certain he is best when Paddy folds, but does not reraise B, in order to keep everyone in. Ricky, with his bad eight low showing, doesn't look too happy, but he also calls. A is distinctly nervous about his three jacks and feels he ought to fold, but having gone so far, he can't quit now. The pot is touching $4,500.

A can hardly believe his luck when the final hole card is dealt. He catches the case jack for four of a kind. He checks because he is sure the low man will bet the hand for him. B, however, is not totally convinced he is best, since he lacks the deuce for the perfect low. Nothing fazed, Ricky weighs in with a final bet of $1,000. This taps the table. (Everyone is playing $1,000 behind, which is, of course, far too much for young men, but boys will be boys.) A has no fears with his four jacks. B, when all is said and done, can't put down a six-five. C, with a full house queens, now doubts if he is good, but as last caller comes in for the "value."

A	(J ♠ J ♦) J ♥ 4 ♦ 8 ♦ 2 ♦ (J ♣)
B	(A ♠ 5 ♣) 3 ♦ 4 ♣ 7 ♣ 6 ♦ (K ♣)
C	(Q ♥ Q ♣) 2 ♥ Q ♦ A ♥ 2 ♣ (10 ♦)
Ricky	(? ?) 4 ♥ A ♣ 8 ♥ 7 ♥ (?)

Now comes the declaration, no coin for low, one coin for high, and two coins for both ways; and if you call both, you have to win both outright, not tie, to take the pot. Everyone juggles nervously with his coins under the table, and Ricky, looking at the array of hands in front of each man around the table, announces that he is *thinking* of going both ways. "Shall I, shan't I? Well . . . in for a penny . . ." and up comes his hand with two coins in it.

"I've only got a six-five for the low," he says.

"Six-five what?" demands B. "I'm six-five, too."

Ricky looks at his hole cards before turning them over. "Six-five-four-two-one," he says.

"That's good," replies B, reluctantly turning down his 6-5-4-3-A.

Now it depends on the high. A looks across to Ricky. "Bad luck," he says, "I've got four of a kind," and he spreads his jacks.

Ricky turns his own cards, showing in the hole 6 ♥ 5 ♥ and 2 ♠. "I've hit a straight flush," he says, not raising his voice by a millimeter. Sitting there like a message written in blood is

4-5-6-7-8, all hearts, with his A ♣ and 2 ♠ for the low hand. Everyone is stunned as Ricky rakes in the chips—$8,400 and a pile of small change—and starts stacking them up.

There is a bit of an inquest: "Why did you raise so much on your three spades and then fold?" someone asks Paddy. This was the raise that threw all the betting out of gear and made it so expensive.

"Jesus, a flush is a good hand at this game!" Paddy retorts.

"Your deal, I think?" chimes in Ricky, and the game goes on. Nothing much happens the rest of the night and Ricky winds up winning all the money.

These things happen, of course, at least in poker romance, but later that day A, B, and C meet for a drink and ask each other: "Can these things actually happen in real life? Surely they can't happen!" And they go over the hand again, analyzing the betting. One puzzle is why Paddy should raise his flush so strongly. All the other bets more or less figure, but that kind of raise doesn't make sense from such an apparently conservative player, unless it's to build the pot up for Ricky. Then suddenly someone recalls an obvious point, which up till now no one had registered. Paddy shuffled and Ricky cut, so no one else handled the cards in the deal.

Well, we know what happened in *The Sting* when the deck was switched . . . but that was a movie. Can anyone pull that kind of thing *seriously?* Wait a moment . . . some guy rang the front-door bell during the evening, apparently wanting to play, and Ricky shooed him away, although there were only five players. Why was that? It begins to look funny. Still the evidence is all circumstantial, it's not proof of a fix. So what about all those strange calls Ricky was in the habit of making at cutthroat. Hadn't that already raised suspicions? True, but suspicion is one thing; conviction beyond a reasonable doubt—sufficient to stop a check at the bank—is another thing.

It's difficult to take it any further. We pay our debts in our

game like gentlemen, dammit. Anyway, who was Paddy
O'Fixit? Someone must know something about him. He must
be known around town. In New York as in London or any big
city, there is always a link between gambling and crime.
There has to be because the two go together like a horse
and a carriage. It's like a spectrum: At one end you have private games among friends in their own homes, which shade
into gambling in smart clubs uptown, which shade into less-
smart clubs downtown and sleazy joints in the backstreets,
which in turn shade into the other end of the scale, organized
crime and the protection racket. That's the way it goes. It's
very useful to have some point of contact with this nether
world, some acquaintance who can tell you what's what, in order to know the score.

     Although I was not involved in Paddy's big deal, as a friend
of the court, as it were, I was "deputed" to investigate the case.
And in one of those cellars where the boys spiel the hours away,
a dim little joint where daylight had never, ever, been known
to penetrate, I told a man about Paddy and the big hand. He
recognized his description right away and asked only one question. "Did he have a coat or a loose jacket on when he dealt?"
He did. "Oh, yes, that's old Golden Fingers!" Golden Fingers?
Golden Fingers.

     After that, the moral problem was significantly eased. A, B,
and C went back to Ricky and confronted him. He blustered
and prevaricated. It turned out, though, that his own record
was not exactly spotless. There had been "coups" before.
Paddy was having a bit of trouble with the law as well. A
and C stopped their checks at the bank, although they had
some anxious moments in case the heavy mob might be
brought in for collection purposes. B, who was straight as a
die himself but a less confident personality, claimed that one
could never be absolutely sure about these things, and that
thinking it over again he had decided the deal was honest. He

let his check go through. So on the night Ricky made a profit after all.

Later analysis of the deal showed the following breakdown. The odds of Ricky being dealt an ace of any suit, a two of a different suit, and four to the eight of any suit save that of the two come out at 3.6 in 10 million, or 1 in 2.8 million. Given that Ricky's hand had been dealt, the odds of four other players receiving hands of which one was four jacks or better, another a full house queens or better, the third A-3-4-5-6 but not a flush, and the fourth being a flush are just over 1 in 1,000 million.

The odds against the whole setup are 4.5 in 10 quadrillion, that is, 4.5 in 10,000,000,000,000,000.

Ricky didn't call back.

CHAPTER TEN

Morals

The game exemplifies the worst aspects of capitalism that have made our country so great.

—WALTER MATTHAU

A fine line is drawn between the status of amateur and professional at poker. Really, it's a moral line. How far do you go, how much do you play, how much do you want to win? There is no doubt that a good player will always win in the long run, and a *very* good player, a master, can win virtually as he pleases in most games, excepting the occasional night when the cards fall badly or his judgment is faulty.

One of the interesting sidelights of Amarillo Slim's account of his poker-playing career in *Play Poker to Win* is the extraordinary but quite matter-of-fact confidence he displays that he *will* win. There are three conditions he requires to be sure of winning when sitting down at a new game, and none of them has anything to do with the cards as such. Here he is in Venezuela: "The three main facts I need to know before I can get down to work: I know that it's a good game—by that I mean a high game; I know I'll get my money if I win; and I know that if some of these cats are going to be losers, I'll get their eyeballs," that is, they will stick all their money in when they get involved in a serious game. Notice the word "work" above. Somehow you can't imagine a professional saying he is getting down to play. Play = work.

The amateur has to avoid being trapped by this formula. Of course the pros do not win all the time. Like Pug Pearson, Slim admits there are times when "you get busted flat on your ass: nobody is *always* a winner, and anybody who says he is, is either a liar or doesn't play poker." The prudent pro in Vegas invests some of his winnings, on the way up, in real estate or some other cash business, so that when the bad days come he isn't left flat. He can borrow money, start up in the little games, get his confidence back, and graduate to the high action again.

The professional games are certainly high—six figures is what "high" means. But the high action comes and goes; it isn't available on tap the whole year round. The inner circle of pros in the United States will travel halfway across the world if they hear of a high game with a seat open. Australia, Latin America, or London, where Slim and Johnny Moss had barely checked into the Hilton when two powerful-looking gentlemen with tight little smiles on their faces came knocking at the door of their room. They didn't carry guns but they made their intentions unmistakably clear.

In order to play in London, they informed the visitors, it will be necessary to cut in the people they represent for 25 percent. Moss blew his top at this announcement, but Slim listened to the proposition more carefully. Then they happened to mention what for him were the magic words: "They guarantee that I'll get any money that I win." That is one of the essential conditions for a "good game," especially for a country boy, as Slim likes to consider himself, in a foreign land. Moss went home, but Slim, though he does not approve of such people and their activities, took out the insurance policy. "Looking at the overall picture, seventy-five percent of the pie looks better to me than no pie at all." Such are the hazards of the professional circuit.

It's a long way, this kind of life, from the Tuesday-night poker games in your hometown. All the same, there is a link between the two and it relates to winning. The danger lies in getting too involved. The fullest endorsement of the philosophy of winning as much as you can, by whatever means you can, short of cheating, is set out by Dr. Frank R. Wallace in *The Advanced Concepts of Poker*. This analytical but some- how slightly manic book is dedicated to the proposition that anyone can win $1,000,000 from his neighbors by applying the right principles. That figure is not chosen at random. The hero of the book, one John Finn (any relation to Mickey?), who is described as a "social worker," won $54,000 playing poker in 1965. He played fifty times in the main game on Mondays, seven times in a minor game to make new contacts on Tues- days, ten times in a similar game on Thursdays, and forty- eight times in an intermediate game on Fridays. "By main- taining the above system of games, he will earn over $1,000,000 from poker in the next twenty years." Maybe so, but my ques- tion is: What kind of social work do you do, John?

Finn is the personification of the all-out, no-holds-barred, skin-'em-alive winner. It's not so much what he does *at* the games, though we'll come to that, it is his conduct *between* the games that is so Machiavellian. While posing as the true and sympathetic friend of the boys, he is nursing them along like a gamekeeper tending a brood of baby pheasants. When they are ready . . . BANG!

His "non-game behavior" includes exaggerating the per- formance of players to their friends, letting people know what a sociable game it is and how easy to win, and flattering the skill of a weak player to his family. If they in turn complain about the player's losses, Finn suggests that the loser's luck is due to change. He makes a point of buttering up the wives. To soothe them, he recalls their husbands' past winnings (and convinces one lady that at least the game keeps her husband from drinking).

Organizing the game, Finn usually has someone else call the big losers, thus avoiding the impression that he is anxious for losers to play. If a new player looks as if he would be a finan- cial asset, Finn keeps him in the game by being friendly and looking after him. Knowing that the new player will lose many thousands of dollars if he becomes a permanent member of the game, Finn sits next to him the first time he plays to guide him through. Whenever he himself is out of a hand, he studies the new man's hand and gives him good advice, so the man's confidence increases and he has a winning night. Conversely, if a new player shows up who looks as if he would be a real threat, Finn drives him out of the game, either by not inviting him again or, if necessary, by insulting him in some way. He is particularly solicitous of the big losers (his raw materials); in fact, his whole approach to the game could be reduced to the single principle: *keep the losers happy.* Because what he is actually doing is running a league system. He organizes minor games at different levels of stakes throughout the week to coach suitable players for the major game at the highest stakes, which is his main source of income—a sort of baseball farm system. For the major game depends on a steady supply of players, all or almost all of whom, in the inevitable nature of things, will be losers.

How to keep them in the game when they are dropping all their money week after week? Finn nurses their egos, protects them from personal comments that could hurt their feelings, resolves all difficulties, deals with credit, etc. He tries to gear the betting to help them win occasionally and—a novel interpretation, this—settles any disputes over the rules in their favor. He helps others in this very Christian way "only to the extent that he can profit." Sympathy and understanding, he finds, can keep the losers going indefinitely; alternatively he may suggest that they move down to a lower stakes game for a while. After suffering sharp losses, some players develop harmful attitudes, such as demanding lower stakes. Finn talks to them privately about their troubles; this has a therapeutic effect. (Well, he is a "social worker," isn't he?) When Finn has an off day for some reason or feels ill, he may skip the game or, better still, turn up, knowing he will not play at his top form, thus altering the consistency of his play. Then if he loses, he will advertise his loss to maximum effect. Even if he misses the game, he will help organize it beforehand to maintain continuity.

Probably all consistent winners apply some of these practices more or less consciously. Certainly if someone is a big loser, everyone throws him a life line to retrieve his battered confidence with that feeblest of all alibis, "Tough luck, you had terrible cards all night." (Bad cards can hit one, of course, but I would estimate that 98 percent of my own losing nights have been a result of bad play, and nothing else.) What sets Finn apart is that he applies these kinds of social-psychological aids to winning with such studied and comprehensive ruthlessness. Yet the whole time, he is playing the outward part of a jolly good fellow, one of the boys.

All this, however, is only a preparation for his technique at the table itself. His system is founded on what must be counted an admirable quality, mental discipline. "The object of poker is to win maximum money. Poker is not a card game; it is a game of money management. Cards are merely the tools for manipulating money." The major enemy of poker players is their rationalization for their failure to think. They continually find excuses for their weaknesses (belief in luck) and lack of self-control.

Their losses are directly proportional to their mental laziness. Finn, on the other hand, uses his mind, the whole time, above all in practicing deception, not just in the strategic sense that his every thought and action are directed toward controlling the game over all, but in the detailed play of the cards.

Here is the story of the $750 sandwich, to serve as an awful warning against lack of discipline.

At draw, one of the players in Finn's game opens $25 on a

pair of aces, is raised to $50, and calls. "Nervous hunger" seizes him; he rushes to the food table and rapidly piles slabs of ham and cheese into a giant sandwich. In the meantime, someone draws a card and flashes an ace, and the dealer, waving the deck around, exposes the bottom card, which is also an ace. (The opener doesn't see it because he is stuffing pickles into his sandwich.)

Hurriedly, he returns to the table, and with mustard-covered fingers, he picks up his cards. The pair of aces is still there but he also has four spades. What to do? Not having seen the flashed aces, he draws three cards. First off the deck, as it happens, is the K ♠, which would have given him a flush. No matter, he makes two pairs, aces and kings, a good enough hand to keep him in for a $50 bet and then a $50 raise. And then he loses to a queen-high flush. "What rotten luck," he complains, finishing off his sandwich. Rotten luck? thinks Finn. If he had stayed at the table instead of gorging himself, he would have seen the two flashed aces and drawn to his four flush to win a $600 pot instead of losing $150 (the ham-and-cheese sandwich cost him $750 bucks). "Also [and this is a characteristic detail], John Finn uses the mustard stains on the cards to identify them in future hands."

Finn is not a cheat, it must be emphasized, in any way. He will take no advantage in the game that is not open to any other player there. He would never steal from the pot, still less fix the cards. He doesn't need to. But if cards become marked in play, he registers the fact and makes use of it.

Discipline is the means to thinking. Finn never wastes time slowly looking at or squeezing his cards; his mind is working on the game, trying to understand what's going on, thinking of his next moves. "*Analytical* thinking is necessary to understand and predict the actions of the opponents. *Objective* thinking is necessary to plan the proper action."

Still more important is control. When Finn has mastered his

own emotions through discipline and understands his opponents through thinking, he can then take *control* of the game. "When in control, he becomes the center of attention. His opponents spend a major portion of their effort trying to figure out his moves and adjusting to them . . . they play according to his actions." From this controlling position he can influence the betting, force opponents into mistakes, and dilute their attention so as to play them off one against the other. He does not go for maximum investment odds on every bet, but mixes up his play—underbetting, overbetting, unexpected and unusual bets—in order to keep his favorable edge, which is the key to his dominance of the game. As a result, confusion and fear decrease the ability of the other players to think objectively and to play their hands correctly. Finn confuses, shocks, bullies, frightens, and worries them.

One example will suffice to demonstrate his dominance. In a draw hand, the pot is opened for $25. Finn, who has been dealt a pair of aces, notices that one of the other players is fumbling with his money, a sure sign that he wants to raise. How can he prevent the raise, to keep the odds favorable and maintain the initiative?

He throws dust in their eyes with a raise of $3.

The would-be raiser drops the money he was fingering. "What's Finn up to?" he demands. "Probably hoping for a raise." Exactly the reaction Finn wanted. Everyone just calls and waits anxiously for his next move. He thus blocks the raise and assumes the offensive betting position.

After the draw, Finn improves to aces up. The danger man looks at his one-card draw. Ha! He had Finn beaten all the time, he grunts; he should've raised him out of his seat. This is a convenient statement for Finn, since it seems to confirm that this player still has only two pairs. He also reads a second man, knowing his betting habits, for two pairs, while a third one-card buyer squeezes his hand slowly and then flings it

away in disgust: he missed his flush. Finn makes a nominal bet
of $1. The first two-pairs player, who has been bluffed by Finn
earlier in the game, reacts emotionally. "You ain't getting off
cheap this time," he tells Finn and raises $50. The second
player hesitates a long time before calling, indicating that he
has only two pairs as well. And Finn, having kept the offensive
position throughout the hand, raises to $100. They call and
lose. By control of the betting, Finn has won the pot with a
normally unfavorable hand and position; and by control of the
players, he has built a potential $100 pot into $400.

Enough is enough: the "advanced concepts" are not empty
phrases. They work, or they certainly should work if the losing
players have sufficient means to keep going until Finn has
stashed his $1,000,000 in the bank. But granted the analysis of
"control" is light-years ahead of any other poker manual,
there is something basically wrong with the thesis. That de-
fect is a moral one. It is not the total deception that the good
player is advised to practice that rankles. At the table, deception is the name of the game, for any winner. Away from the
table . . . well, some degree of encouragement of the losers
is obviously right and proper. Nor is it merely the degree of
deception required that one objects to, that it goes too far.

What is wrong is that application of Finn's principles in
their fullest form would leave time for nothing else. It is not
hard to see that Finn's life is filled with poker. Wife, children,
home, they don't get a mention; not even a girl friend. Those
nights of the week when he is not playing poker it is hard to
imagine him doing anything else but thinking about the game,
keeping his notebooks up to date, rehearsing new stratagems.
All right, a million dollars is a million dollars, even over twenty
years in these inflationary times. But what's it for? To what
use will the million be put? It won't enhance his life-style; it
can't, because he hasn't *got* any life. One is tempted to conclude that devotion to winning on such a scale is itself patho-

logical, that compulsive winning is as self-destructive in its way as compulsive losing.

The "moral" problem of gambling, as it was usually understood, virtually disappears under the pragmatic gaze of modern Christian theologians. Traditionally, there have been two arguments about gambling. One, that gambling was wrong in itself, which was broadly the Protestant view in England; and two, that gambling was wrong only if taken to excess, which was the Catholic position. The outcome of this argument, according to Rev. Gordon Moody, director of the Churches' Council on Gambling in London, was "a dead draw." Morally speaking, neither argument was conclusive.

But what was more significant about this debate was that neither side checked out its assumptions with the behavior of gamblers themselves. For what their conduct reveals is that motives are often quite other than monetary gain (see Chapter Six).

For instance, people attempting to gain the greatest financial reward, like winning a lottery, devote least attention to gambling; whereas gamblers who concentrate on their betting and get great excitement or satisfaction from gambling, like people spending the afternoon in an off-track betting parlor, are in reality less concerned with money than excitement. In other words, the churches' moral position was based on a misunderstanding of what gambling is all about, and how gamblers are motivated.

Gambling exists in virtually all societies in different guises. What is excess? Answer: It all depends on the individual. It follows that in modern society the chief concern should not really be a moral one, trying to decide what degree of gambling is moral or immoral; rather it should be a social concern, to insure that gambling takes place in properly controlled ways. The moral point, if you will, is reversed: it consists in insuring that those who profit from organized gambling—casino operators et al.—should not take unfair advantage of the public.

In Jewish tradition (Mishnah Sanhedrin 3:1) the professional gambler is among those disqualified from witnessing. The reasons given by the commentators are that he doesn't benefit society and that, inasmuch as he takes advantage of the weakness and ill luck of others, he is akin to a robber. Modern Jewish teaching, however, would differentiate between forms of gambling from the plainly objectionable to the seemingly harmless. According to Rabbi John Rayner, the degree of gravity diminishes to the extent to which (a) the game involves skill as well as chance; (b) the stakes are small; (c) the beneficiary is a charity rather than the individual player; (d) the game is only a subsidiary part of the evening's entertainment; and (e) the primary motive is the companionship that the game provides (especially for lonely people) rather than the titillation of the gambling instinct. This humane classification seems to me eminently sensible for anyone who seeks a moral frame for his gambling activities (or, for that matter, for any authority concerned with regulating gaming).

In an addendum to Finn's poker career, Dr. Wallace seems to anticipate the objection that compulsive winning is as destructive as compulsive losing. "While it is obvious that poker losers are self-made fools for not using their minds, perhaps the biggest fool is the good player. With his efficacious mind and willingness to exert effort, he is profligating [sic] his most precious possession . . . his time . . . time needed to pursue expanded, long-range goals that he is capable of achieving." Poker is a nonproductive activity. One must assume, from experience if not on moral grounds, that happiness and fulfillment are based on a life aimed, in some way, at productive achievement. Or as Dr. Wallace puts it, "the good player may be the biggest loser in the game," that is, he is capable of using his abilities to greater purpose than winning at poker.

Every player has to decide for himself his degree of involvement, how much time he should devote to playing and, therefore, how much he wants to win or can afford to lose. Poker differs from almost all other games because it is about money. Money, so to speak, is how you keep the score. (The same goes for backgammon.) You may be mad about golf or tennis or chess, but you do not make money at these games, unless you bet on the result, and even then the return for time expended is likely to be very small indeed. Because poker is a direct, untaxed, continuing, and extremely valuable way of capitalizing leisure time, there is far more of a temptation to exploit the opportunities it offers, to substitute poker for life itself.

It is a curious thing about money. A man is prepared to bet $5 or $50, or it may be $500 or more, on a bluff on a valueless hand, see it vanish faster than the snows of yesteryear when beaten by a stronger hand, and scarcely blink an eyelash. Yet at dinner before the game, the same man may object to paying $2.50 for what he considers an overpriced shrimp cocktail, and demand that the head waiter amend his bill at once. How does one reconcile these two attitudes? Frankly, I don't think one can. All you can say is that gambling money, somehow or other, seems different. You may lose the bluff, but it's an investment, dammit, not a losing bet, and you'll get it back later, with interest. Whereas the shrimp cocktail is gone forever down the alimentary canal. If you try to win a million dollars at poker, you won't have time for anything else; and by the time you've won the money, you won't be fit for anything else.

A professional poker player is something else again. Unlike Finn, who is acting out a part, pretending to be an amateur when he is in reality subordinating everything else to winning, a professional has made a choice of career. Men like Pug Pearson, Amarillo Slim, and Johnny Moss appear to have, in their own way, rounded lives: families, friends, leisure activities fit into the pattern. Everyone knows where they stand and what they are, and there is a comradeship among such people, as in any professional group. Even so, Pug Pearson, who is generally acknowledged by other pros to be the best all-round player in action, sometimes has doubts about his life. He tends to hanker for something more worthwhile, attributing his way of life as a card player and hustler, maybe with justification, to his lack of opportunity and formal education. The sons of such masters do not follow their fathers' profession. But that is not to deny, for the rest of us, that poker is the best thing yet discovered for profitable amusement.

CHAPTER ELEVEN

Ends and Odds

"How long does it take to learn poker, Dad?"
"All your life, son."
—MICHAEL PERTWEE

At poker there aren't any rules strictly applied and codified as in other games. Instead, there's a general consensus about how the game is played, modified by all sorts of little local rulings and understandings that each poker gathering introduces for itself.

Remember the old story about the new man in a poker game who gets involved in a huge hand of draw? After a swinging series of raises and reraises, the hand is finally shown down.

"Four bullets!" announces the new player gleefully, reaching out with both hands to the mound of chips in the pot.

"Hold it a moment!" protests the other big raiser. "I've got the immortal hand," and he spreads the 2 ♦ 4 ♦ 6 ♦ and a one-eyed jack and a one-eyed king across the baize. "That beats everything else in this game!"

The newcomer stifles his curses manfully, throws his four aces into the discards, and plays on. Later that night, by a happy chance, he's dealt the same hand pat, 2 ♦ 4 ♦ 6 ♦ and a one-eyed jack and king. He bets it up, takes every raise, and triumphantly spreads his hand out. "How about that?" he crows.

"Two pairs here," says another player calmly, seizing the pot from him.

"Wha'd'ya mean! This is the immortal hand, and it beats everything else in this game, right?"

The winner gazes at him in amazement. *"Only before mid-night."*

The moral of which story is: Always ask what the rules are before you sit down in a new game.

The reason there are no absolutely fixed rules is that poker is a living and growing kind of game, not subject to a central ruling body that sets standards for players as a whole. It is more of a private battle adapted to the personal whims of those who choose to wage it.

The original authority on card games was, of course, the English lawyer Edmond Hoyle (1672–1769), whose fame has been so magnified over the years that his name has passed into the language in the expression "according to Hoyle."

The only snag so far as poker is concerned is that Hoyle died some sixty years before the game made its appearance. So if someone says in support of a ruling or to settle an argument, "According to Hoyle . . ." it is only a way of saying according to the rules as generally laid down or codified by some contemporary authority.

Indeed, the curious thing about poker is that the "rules" of draw, the classic game, can be learned in a couple of minutes. Once the order of hands has been set out, from a straight flush down to a pair, there simply isn't anything much to learn about the "rules." You get dealt five cards and make the opening bets, draw new cards, and bet the hand out. And that's it, pardner. It's probably because poker is such a simple game, in its mechanics, that so many players think they know all there is to it and attribute their losses to bad luck. Whereas it takes a long, long time to master draw poker.

No need here to rehearse the whole corpus of rules as set out by latter-day experts who have made their compilations at length. (Messrs. George Coffin and Albert Morehead's is probably the standard version.) A quasi-legal code may have some value in settling disputes, but all real players already know as

The Innovation

much about the rules as is necessary; or as one of the old jazz men said when asked to explain rhythm, "If you has to ask what it is, you ain't got it."

What is more worthwhile is to take a look at how the main variations of poker differ, illustrating the theme by some tables of odds. Actually, there are so many variations of poker, going under different local names, that I doubt whether any definitive list can be made. The point is that once you've got the basics clear, you can straighten out any new variation you may bump into one dark night.

One golden rule applies to every form of poker, though it is neglected by players again and again, which is that if you start with the best hand, you are likely to end up with the best hand. Simple mathematics, after all.

But this golden rule, this cornerstone, is qualified by two other considerations. One, the second-best or lesser hands may improve to beat the best hand; two, most of the time you never know, and the others don't know either, whether you really have the best hand to start with.

Your estimate of your cards, therefore, is measured against the probability of the average hand that would be dealt in a given situation.

TABLE I
PROBABILITIES OF GETTING A PAT HAND

One pair will be dealt out in every 2.4 hands.
Two pairs will appear once in 21 hands.
Three of a kind once in 47 hands.
A straight once in 255 hands.
A flush once in 509 hands.
A full house once in 694 hands.
Four of a kind once in 4,165 hands.
A straight flush once in 72,193 hands.
A royal straight flush once in 649,740 hands.

This in turn is the basis of the tried and trusty principle of *draw:* In a five-handed game you need at least jacks to open. Holding jacks you will be as good or better than anyone else in just under half the hands you play (47%); holding queens this will be true in just over half the hands (54%). In a seven-handed game the distribution of cards leads to a higher average hand, so you need aces or at least kings to feel confident about opening under the gun. Sitting farther around the table, this holding can be shaded, because the assumption is that if the earlier players do not open they do not hold aces or kings (leaving aside the possibility that someone is sandbagging); so in third or fourth seat, queens or jacks may be best; sitting one from last, a small pair may be good enough. Good enough for what? To be the best hand at the table, at that point.

That doesn't mean to say that you're going to win with sevens or sixes, of course. Someone ahead of you may be checking with a full house; others will be sitting on four flushes or open-ended straights. But it is a fair assumption that you are nominally best and can (if you want to) take the initiative. It's not recommended too often; but the others don't know you're not sitting on aces.

This applies to draw when a player who checks can come back in if it's opened farther around the table. In those club games where after the dealer antes (or the next player puts up a blind opener), each successive player has to call or throw his hand in, relative strength according to position is more reliable. It risks being too expensive for the fourflushers and straighteners to open as opposed to backing in cheaply. Sitting last in this kind of draw game, a low pair or even an ace-king can be strong; the reason is that there is only one man to beat—and he was a "blind" opener.

The idea of *jackpots* in draw—no one being allowed to open

unless he has a pair of jacks or better—is to keep the game
"true," so that it is played on the basis of the average hand as
it is dealt before the draw. Jackpots offers less scope for betting and bluffing than straight draw, in which you can open
on anything and let the others decide whether you've really
got what you're supposed to have; but it has the compensating
advantage of building up bigger pots. If it isn't opened, everyone chips in for a *queenpot;* and if that isn't opened, it goes on
up to a *kingpot* and an *acepot.* And if it still isn't opened,
which sometimes happens, the requirement descends from
acepot back to the original jacks. As the pot builds up, in a
limit game, the ante may offer good value for almost any
draw.

So the next important table of probabilities concerns improvement. You have to measure the odds against improving
your hand in the draw against the value in money terms of the
pot. That is, if the odds of hitting a flush are 4 to 1 and the pot
is offering you better odds than that, say 50 chips for a call of
5, and you think if you hit your flush you will win, you are onto
a good bet. If the pot is offering you less, say 10 chips for a call
of 5, it's a bad bet. Elementary, my dear Watson. But can you
cross your heart and say you know the difference in the odds
between, say, holding a pair with an ace kicker and drawing
to an inside straight?

Although the chances that a player will be dealt specified
hands at poker are well known, the chance of being in a position to open a jackpot is too complicated to be dealt with exactly by theoretical analysis. In a study conducted at Birming-
ham University (England) in 1967, an electronic computer
was used which could simulate poker hands at a rate of 7,000
a minute. (Playing one night a week you might be dealt something like 5,000 hands in a year.)

The machine found, in a run of 150,000 deals, that the
chances of opening a jackpot rose from 0.374 (roughly 5 to 3

against) in a two-handed game to 0.502 (even money) for three players, increasing to 0.612 (8 to 5 in favor) for four players, and to 0.694 (7 to 3 in favor) for five.

TABLE II

ODDS AGAINST IMPROVING IN THE DRAW

One pair drawing three cards	any improvement	5–2
" "	to two pairs	5–1
" "	to trips	8–1
" "	to a full house	97–1
" "	to fours	360–1
One pair and a kicker drawing two cards	any improvement	3–1
" " "	to two pairs	5–1
" " "	to trips	12–1
" " "	to a full house	120–1
One pair and an ace drawing two cards	to aces up	7–1
" " "	to other two pairs	15–1
Two pairs drawing one card	to a full house	11–1
Three of a kind drawing two cards	any improvement	9–1
" "	to a full house	15–1
" "	to fours	23–1
Threes with a kicker drawing one card	any improvement	11–1
" "	to a full house	15–1
" "	to fours	46–1
Four straight open-ended drawing one card	to a straight	5–1
" inside or one end " "	"	11–1
Four flush drawing one card	to a flush	4–1
Four straight flush open ended " "	to any improvement	2–1
" " " "	to a straight flush	23–1
Four flush inside or one end straight	to a straight or better	3–1
drawing one card	to a straight flush	46–1

This confirms the point that in a game of five players it is not enough to hold just the minimum pair of jacks and it squares with the empirical rule of thumb that in a seven-handed game you need aces to be first to open. As for jacks or queens, they should certainly be checked, and if there is any sign of strength around the table, they should be pitched in before the draw.

What about two small pairs? Remember what your Momma done tole you . . . Never buy insurance from a man with a diamond stickpin; never buy a secondhand car from a man called Doc; and never get hooked by two small pairs. Before the draw you can use them to raise and hope to drive out the opposition, but after the draw they're weak as water. Someone else is going to be drawing to two higher pairs. It's 11 to 1 against your hitting, and even if you do, he may fill too. And then you're skewered.

Draw, more than most variations of poker, requires patience to play well. Poker Alice understood that (see Chapter Six). You've got to be prepared to sit and wait and throw in, sit and wait and throw in, until the cards start coming. They nearly always do. But to increase the action, variations, such as *deuces wild,* were introduced. This elevates the average opening hand to three of a kind, which is easier to hit than two pairs; while after the draw, fours are not uncommon, being easier to hit than a full house or a flush.

The *bug,* or a joker that counts either as an ace or can be used as a card to fill a straight or a flush, is another device to liven up draw, and it changes all the odds radically. The same principles apply to opening and raising, but the scale against which you measure the strength of your hands, because it is so much easier to get good cards, is considerably higher.

As for simplicity, could anything be clearer and cleaner than *five card stud?* One card down and four in turn face up—it's not exactly difficult to learn the rules. Yet it's a great betting game, requiring both judgment and courage in high degree, which explains why it has kept its tremendous popularity wherever poker is played.

Starting with the best hand, as in draw, remains the key;

the only snag is that players disagree sharply about what constitutes the right openers.

TABLE III
PROBABILITIES OF GETTING A PAT HAND WITH DEUCES (OR ANY FOUR OF A KIND) WILD

A pair will be dealt out in every	2.1	hands
Trips will appear once in	7	"
Two pairs " "	27	"
A straight " "	39	"
Four of a kind "	84	"
A flush " "	197	"
A full house " "	205	"
A straight flush "	638	"
Five of a kind "	3,868	"
A royal straight flush "	5,370	"

PROBABILITIES OF GETTING A PAT HAND WITH THE BUG

A pair will be dealt out in every	2.4	hands
Trips will appear once in	21	"
Two pairs " "	23	"
A straight " "	140	"
A flush " "	360	"
A full house " "	438	"
Four of a kind "	920	"
A straight flush "	15,943	"
A royal straight flush "	119,570	"
Five of a kind "	220,745	"

Herbert Yardley advised coming in only on two-card combinations from the ace to the ten, or on ace-x or king-x if no other ace or king is showing; and folding a low pair if the third card fails to give you trips. He went so far as to describe his refusal to draw more than one card to any pair lower than nines as "my greatest contribution to five card stud."

All this seems far too rigid and conservative these days. It often makes sense to come in at stud if no one else is showing a better card than you. It all depends on the price, your position, and the overall situation. The next card may change things in all sorts of ways. "If you're going to stay in the game only on high cards," as Amarillo Slim observes in his usual pithy way, "there is nothing in the world to playing stud, because when you come in you're telling everybody what you've got."

Of course, low pairs in the hole have to be treated circumspectly, and frequently folded, but not always.

There's a parallel between tennis and five card stud, one might suggest. At tennis a player may go for outrageous winners, on the chance that he has his touch that day, especially in the early games of a set; whereas when crucial points are being played later in the match, the same man will rely strictly on the safe "percentage" shots. In stud, in the early part of the session, you may well play fast and loose to test your form and, if possible, get the opposition running; but as play settles down, you will normally revert to sound values.

Suppose you are dealt (7)-7 wired and there are kings and queens showing around the board. You come in and buy an ace. That card is going to terrify the opposition if you bet it.

All right, supposing you don't catch the ace on the third card, but a middling ten. Sitting in a position where no one can raise after you, that is, lower cards than the ten are showing in the hands still to call, you may still have a fair chance. With three other players in, you have seen or know about fifteen cards and there are (you assume) two sevens and three tens left in the deck to help you: 7 to 1 against improving. The point is that if you hit your trips sevens and the kings or queens improve to two pairs, you are going to have them over a barrel.

The effervescent Eric Steiner, who wins money at five card stud like a man shelling peas, once offered this sage advice:

TABLE IV

FIVE CARD STUD ODDS IN A SEVEN-HANDED GAME

Odds against pairing your hole card in the last three cards if no matching card is showing	4–1
" " " if one matching card is showing	6.5–1
" " " if two matching cards are showing	14–1
Odds against catching trips, starting off with a pair, in next three cards if no matching card is showing	6.5–1
" " if one matching card is showing	14–1
Odds against catching a straight starting off with three consecutive cards and no helping cards showing	3.5–1
" " a flush " three cards in suit and no helping cards showing	4–1

"Make up your mind what the other man's hole card is, otherwise he will decide what yours is!"

Here's one instance where I managed to apply this precept. Sitting with (2)-2 against a series of high cards, the last player to speak around the table raised on a jack. As the raise went around, one after another the kings and queens folded. So, what's he got? It could be jacks backed, certainly, but this was a shrewd man against me and I thought he had probably raised on the overlay with an ace in the hole. It's the logical move, sitting last. And it didn't feel like jacks facing me somehow. Next card gave him another high card and I caught a lousy three. He bet the pot.

Now the correct thing here is to believe him and chuck in the cards. But I was convinced he only had the ace. You can argue that my (2)-2-3 have less chance of improving than his (A)-J-10, but that's not the right way to look at it. I don't *need* to improve to win. Of the forty-one unknown cards left, only nine will help him; if he catches any one of the others, my deuces will still stand up. My fourth card was another low one and he still didn't improve. He weighed in with another big bet. I was still convinced he only had the ace and I called. Last card no improvement. At that point he paused a long time and finally checked. I didn't quite have the chutzpa to raise on (2)-2-3-6-8 into four high cards; it was satisfaction enough when he turned the ace over. "Ace in the hole, all the time broke," as they often complain at the National Press Club in Washington.

There are one or two variations at stud, designed to liven things up, such as dealing each card face down and giving the players the option of which one to roll up, sometimes known as Mexican stud. If you catch a low pair, you can show it up, either to restrain the opposition from betting or to bluff trips. On the other hand, as soon as you show an ace, people will get really suspicious. Another device at stud is a buy at the end, a sixth card exchanged either for the hole card or one of the up cards from the original hand; this raises the level of betting considerably but doesn't fundamentally alter the structure of stud.

In London clubs, five card stud with a stripped deck is quite widely played, that is, all the cards from two to six are removed, leaving thirty-two in the deck. (Which is a cue to recall the old gag, "Hey! Fellers! George has dropped dead at the table! What're we gonna do?" "Aw, throw out the deuces and treys.")

Five card stud with a stripped deck is a real pro game; the opportunities for cheating are so manifold—signaling the position of just one card to a confederate can be vital—that it is best avoided unless you are sure of the company. Who knows what some muttered exclamation in Greek or Persian or Arabic may mean? To give the players some protection, the rule at London clubs is English only at the table.

Paradoxically, the key to this game is not so much starting on the best cards (that helps, of course) but adding up the possibilities of improvement. Someone may make aces against you, but if the other two aces have gone and you are sitting on a low pair with live side cards, you can be odds-on to win. For example, in a seven-handed game it comes down to your (10)-10-K-Q on the fourth card against one player with (A)-7-8-A; there are ten cards left in the deck of which (to take an extreme case) eight can improve your hand and none your opponent's; you are the 4 to 1 favorite. (Another quirk of this game, by the way, is that an ace can also count as a 6, to make a bottom straight.)

Seven card stud, also known as Down the River or Seven-Toed Pete, is an altogether different proposition from five card stud. Having two cards in the hole to start with, plus a final card down, means that big hands may on occasion be completely concealed; the average winning hand is around the level of aces up. In any case, you have to read your opponents as best you can, even if the information is to be inferred only by its absence.

As a case in point, here is a hand I was rather proud of winning in a big club game. It was late at night, there were only the hard cases left, and it was more trouble to go to bed than to go on playing. One man who had been bobbing and weaving through the betting all night, opened as high card on a K ♠, which we all called; then he bet strongly on the J ♠. I called again, though I was showing only the 9 ♥ and the 5 ♣. When I failed to show any improvement on the fifth card, he bet the pot at me. The others dropped. This was a tight professional kind of game and that sort of bet was a gauntlet; fold or be prepared to stick your whole stack in.

Now I felt his original bet on K ♠ J ♠ was a semibluff designed to push me out; if he had two spades in the hole, he might well have checked to keep me in; even if he did have them, he hadn't hit his hand yet, so I placed him with a pair of kings maximum, possibly a lower pair.

But the real point of recalling this hand is this: How was he to read me with my rubbish showing? He knew I would not chase his hand with (? ?) 9 ♥ 5 ♣ 2 ♦, not against a hefty pot-sized bet, when he was looking so strong. If I had trips down there I would surely raise him back. So what could I possibly have?

Only one thing in the world I could have, if you think about it, and that was aces wired in the hole. No aces had shown, which was a clue; but a process of elimination should have told him that that was the only realistic holding for me to wade in so far against his overlay.

Sixth card gave us each a medium card, again no visible improvement, and with quite a good pot riding, he bet it all at me. I had about 200 chips left and this virtually tapped me out. I couldn't know, of course, that one of his low cards hadn't given him a second pair to match his kings (if he had kings); but my aces still felt good and a second pair would top him in any case. It takes nerve to stick it all in, because if you lose you're wiped out. You have to raise more money or let someone else waiting around take your seat. But if you don't have the courage of your convictions, you don't deserve charity either, so in the chips went. I peeked nervously at the final hole card—nothing—and turned my single pair of aces. He scowled furiously at his hand and flung the cards across the table. He just had the kings.

The loser, who was a tough gentleman with a short temper, which in fact was responsible for his having spent some considerable time in residence at one of Her Majesty's less agreeable *pensions,* started cursing his luck and turned on the dealer: "You gave him all my cards! Any one of them would have paired me!" "But, Henry," I interposed mildly, "don't blame the dealer, I had the best hand from the start."

Henry ought to have read my aces, but this was also a good example of pricing a hand. If I'd had more money in front of me, I probably wouldn't have won. Having failed to improve the aces on the last card, I doubt if I'd have had the gall to stick in yet another 200. With only a few chips left, what the hell!

Seven card stud is a good, active game that moves along just fast enough to play it all night. It's never easy to handle because there are too many unknowns in the hidden cards. As an exercise to keep alert and to sharpen your game, it's a good idea to try to "place" the hole cards of your opponents in every hand, even when you drop.

Opinions about what to come in on vary quite widely among the experts. The truth of the matter is that it is a mistake to be too inflexible about it. Playing his system (which is fantastically tight), Yardley claims he won 5 times out of 6 and lost on the other occasion only half his average winnings per session. Maybe so. All I can say is that I have never managed to make it pay, though that may be my weakness.

Yardley advises against opening unless you have trips, pairs of aces or kings, three straights and flushes, or any pair with an ace or a king, and adds that a pair of queens should be folded if you don't improve on the fourth card.

To my mind a pair concealed in the hole is, potentially, a devastating hand. It's hard to hit the third one, of course—in a seven-handed game the odds are 10 to 1 against hitting it in the next two cards if no matching cards are showing—but the possibilities for chicanery are far higher than if you show a pair of bullets for all and sundry to admire; that kind of hand merely wins the ante.

Pug Pearson, who is reputedly the best player of seven card stud in the United States, once observed (and he is not a man given to boasting without cause) that he had made more money at seven card stud on a pair of deuces than most people could make on a full house aces.

The following table indicates the odds against hitting various hands at seven card stud, but in a practical way, by making allowance for a given number of cards, including cards to help your hand, showing around the table.

If five card stud is less popular these days among the high rollers in Vegas and other points west, it is because the play tends to clam up, it becomes too mechanical, and there is not enough to go for. Hold 'em, with its electrifying combination of draw and five card stud, has supplanted it.

Each player gets two cards in the hole, followed by a round of betting.

Then three cards, "the flop," are dealt face up in the middle as community cards, followed by a second round of betting.

A fourth card is turned up with another bet and then a fifth card with a final round of betting. You can use any combina-

TABLE V
SEVEN CARD STUD ODDS

Starting with	Odds against improving to at least		Assuming*
One pair and an ace	Aces up	4–3	6 cards showing
″ ″	Three of a kind	4–1	″ ″
Two pairs	Full house	13–5	8 cards showing
Three straight	Straight	3–1	6 cards showing (one helping)
Three flush	Flush	7–2	″ ″ ″
Four straight	Straight	5–4	8 cards showing (one helping)
Four flush	Flush	1–1	″ ″ ″
Three straight and three cards to a flush in four cards	Straight or flush	9–2	8 cards showing (one straight and two flush helping)
Three of a kind and one off card in four cards	Full house	7–5	8 cards showing
Four straight flush	Straight or flush	1–2	8 cards showing (one straight and two flush helping)
″	Straight flush	6–1	8 cards showing

* It obviously makes a big difference what cards are showing in other hands, because the more helping cards out, the harder it becomes to improve a particular hand.

tion of cards from the five in the middle with your own two hole cards to make your hand.

Hole Cards	*Community Cards*
(x x) bet	x x x bet; x bet; x bet

Any number of players from two to ten, and in theory even more, can play hold 'em. While the number of betting intervals is the same as in five card stud and the number of cards the same as in seven card stud, the game is a great deal faster and fiercer than either.

The essence of the challenge at hold 'em is that while it is easy enough to put a value on the first two cards you get in the hole, their real worth depends on the first three up cards dealt in common. Thus the first decision, whether to come in or not, depends on the value of your own hand; but the second decision, which is the crucial one, relates to all the other players' hands.

So what do you start on? Tricky question. What counts is not so much good cards—obviously aces wired is the best hand—but promising *situations;* you have to read the situation, working back from the flop and what the betting tells you about the other hands out.

For starters, there are $\dfrac{52 \times 51}{2} = 1{,}326$ combinations of two cards. That's a pretty wide choice. Any high pair in the hole is useful, A-x in the same suit is very strong, A-x off suit or two honor cards have potential, low pairs can be rewarding. But no hand means anything unless the price is right. If there's a lot of early raising, a medium-sized pair should be stacked. If you get in cheaply, though, you can play on rubbish like (2-7)—why not? For a cheap call, there's little to lose and the up cards might produce three deuces, as once happened to me, against a full house kings. In a true game, where the betting is accurate, the pot will be raised before the draw at least once if not more, as players act to prevent these cheap draws. If it isn't, you can come along for the ride.

To take an extreme case, someone may be holding back on (A-A), but if the flop shows 3 ♠ 4 ♠ 5 ♠ then the best hole cards are the 6 ♠ and the 7 ♠. Whether you judge it's worth getting into the pot on those kinds of cards depends entirely on the level of the opening betting.

The flop is the middle game: it changes everything. Now you can see if there is any chance of a flush or a straight being made, which are very live chances at hold 'em; you can gauge the reaction of the strong raiser to the new cards by the way he bets; and, most important, you can estimate your chances of making the hand you want.

The key to tactics at hold 'em is to treat the first two cards like stud, but the flop like draw, at that stage you have a five card hand to work with; strategically, play the game as a variation of seven card stud. A somewhat complicated admixture, but that's the fascination of hold 'em.

A practical analysis of hold 'em, its figuring and its rationale, is demonstrated by Pug Pearson's play in the world championship (see Chapter Four). This is master-class stuff and highly instructive.

And so to lowball. The trouble with *draw lowball,* or misère, as they used to call it at Crockford's, is that your hand can actually get *worse* on the draw. This never applies at high poker, where if you are dealt a pair, you won't end up with less than the pair (splitting openers to draw to a flush is a different matter); whereas at lowball, you can throw a nine, drawing to a wheel with A-2-3-4, and catch another ace to pair you up.

An interesting comparison: While there are only 664 straight flushes and fours of a kind in the deck, there are 5,120 hands that contain six as the highest card. The frequency of such hands is almost exactly equivalent to holding a flush; in other words, they come up all the time. Good hands in lowball are easier to catch, or easier to hit on the draw, than are good hands at high poker.

If you are dealt a pat nine, its value is roughly equivalent to between jacks up and aces up at draw. It's a useful hand to catch, but not conclusive. The usual technique is to make a heavy raise to drive out the one card buyers and then stand pat. If one man is drawing to A-2-3-4, there are (assuming that straights don't spoil your low) five cards (5, 6, 7, 8, 9) for him to beat you and eight cards (because he may pair up) to ruin him. Those are good odds in your favor, and even if you get burned now and again, you will have a plus score in the long run.

But suppose having raised your pat nine, someone else re-raises. What then? It looks as if he is going to take the 8 to 5 odds when you break your hand, and you may have to reconsider. Clearly, throwing a nine when your next high card is a four is a very different proposition from throwing a nine when your next high card is an eight, because the other man may have your eight beaten at the start. It may be that you have "value" only if a third player is in the pot.

Here's an impressive piece of betting and bluffing at draw lowball involving two world champions, Pug Pearson and Johnny Moss.

It was deuce to the seven, known as Kansas City lowball, and Pug found 2-3-4-7-J in his hand. There was a full table, $200 ante, and after the first round of betting, two other players were left in.

The man on Pug's right bet $1,000; Pug raised (it's obvious) to try to drive out Moss behind him, and made a bet of $2,800; but Moss called and raised again, another $5,000. The first man, who was a tight player, just called the raises.

Now, at this point, Pug reckoned this man either had a perfect hand or else he had to draw a card, and it was 100 to 1 (near enough) that he did not have the cinch. So he stuck it all in, about $25,000, to force Moss out and either buy the pot outright or get the 8 to 5 advantage in his favor.

Moss knew, of course, that Pug had a hand, but what kind of a hand? It was not the perfect seven low; more likely he read him—knowing him from a myriad other games—as a ten or a jack low. He called because he figured he's getting 2 to 1 for his money when the first player backs in. But here came something he hadn't bargained for: the third man dropped. Pug's reraise was evidently too high for him to risk it. Moss was getting only about 6 to 5 for his money then, which was not the same investment at all.

If the third man had stayed in, Pug would have been forced to throw his jack. But with only one player to beat, he stood pat, trying to make Moss draw instead.

Moss knew this wasn't a bluff, in the sense that all the money was in. The hand was going to be shown down whatever happened. He stalled; he probably put Pug with a nine or perhaps an eight low; and he decided he had to draw. He discarded his high card, which was a *ten*.

And now Pug's jack was clear favorite. Only four low cards or another ten would win for Moss; the remaining eight cards lose.

Pug flipped over his hand as Moss drew and told him, "Johnny, you made a mistake; now beat that jack." Moss looked at his draw: a king. "Oh, my God, I dumped the winning hand."

He didn't play the hand badly; he was outplayed. This is play at the master level, a combination of psychology, position, and odds, what Pug means by playing a "fine line."

Drawing one card only is the standard procedure at five card lowball, but there are occasions when a two or even a three card draw is justified. Sitting last, with three or four players calling the opener, the money odds make a long shot worth trying. But if someone can raise you back before the draw, it's too reckless.

Seven card low (the reverse of the high version) is not a very strong game because straights, flushes, and full houses don't come into the reckoning, and if someone is showing best, he automatically bets the pot. It becomes too mechanical and too expensive to try to outdraw. In limit games, such as they play in Vegas, second-best hands can call; but at table stakes, no one is going to stick around with higher cards showing.

Pug once remarked that he thought seven card low, *razz*, as it's known, contained only about 2 percent skill. As this was the game I used to play most when on flying visits to Vegas, I felt somewhat put down. The technique, playing limited raises, is that you stick around until you get three low cards dealt and avoid getting involved otherwise. It's important to remember that it's the *second*-highest card in your low hand that matters in trying to outdraw a better low.

Someone may be looking down your throat with (?-?)-3-8-9-10 against your (A-2)-3-7-Q-K. He hasn't really got you strangled despite your higher cards. The point is that, if you both improve, you are drawing to a seven and he is drawing to an eight. Not only is any bet at limit stakes worth calling, but if you have seen that the low cards you need are not out, and that the cards he probably needs have fallen, you have distinct chances.

The curious feature of razz as played in Vegas is that the *high* card has to open the pot, which frequently means you are throwing in $10 or $20 or $30, depending on the level of the game, on a king, queen, or jack—a "paint," as a cook I knew there used to call these court cards. Normally someone showing a low card is going to raise the opening bet, to establish his position, and you can throw your high card in without further loss. But sometimes, dealt, say, (A-2)-K against eights or nines or only one good hand, you can have a try at it.

I remember this cook (I hope he baked better than he staked) because in just such a hand I had a row at the table over his play one day. He had drawn something like (?-?)-6-7-J-("Paint!")-Q-("Paint again!") and rose to his feet with a snort—maybe he had an appointment in the kitchen—instructing his next-door neighbor at the table to play out the hand for him.

"But you can't do that!" I shrilled, my English accent rising an octave in protest. "You can't have someone else play your hand for you!" I was sitting on a jack low myself and was scared of being outdrawn on the last card. All eyes turned to me, this weirdo who was shouting at the table. The poker manager looked up, one of those beefy, jowly operators you see all over town, and padded over from his desk in the center of the room.

"Deal the card!" he ordered the dealer. The cook was still several paces away from the table, watching disgustedly. I peeked at my hole card; it was a bad one again. "Who's playing this hand?" I demanded. "I check it!"

The manager turned over the cook's card, which was another paint. "Don't worry," he admonished me somberly, "there ain't nuthin' to this game but luck anyways."

That was not quite accurate but it did make me feel that my continued presence at the table was not going to prove the contrary.

A variation that can lead to more action, because more players can get involved, is seven card low with kings wild.

Five card stud low has not got much point: best low is going to bet the maximum automatically in case he gets paired.

Some London clubs play a variation of seven card high or seven card low where instead of all the cards being dealt out in the normal way, the sixth and then the seventh cards are changed for one of your hole cards or an up card, or if your hand is already made, you stand pat.

Thus playing lowball with (A-K)-2-3-6, you would bet and change the hole card; if you catch another high card or a pair, you have another chance to change on the seventh. In a concealed hand like this you have the initiative; whereas changing an up card, say (A-2)-3-4-K, is far less dominating because everyone can see what you're getting. On a pat eight, say (A-2)-3-7-8, against a man buying to lower cards, say

(?-?)-2-3-K, you would probably stand pat and hope for the best. If he draws a low card, you have to decide whether it has paired him in the hole or not.

This variation of seven card stud is a good one, with plenty of chances for bluffing. The tactical point is to bet the pot up early in the hand. If you have (A-K)-2 or even (9-8)-7, you want to drive out the opposition and then stand pat. The rule is, though, that if you don't exchange a card on the sixth, you can't take one on the seventh either.

Up to now we've been talking about high *or* low games, but hi-lo is where the action is. There are so many ways of reversing or disguising your hand or steering through to a winning ending that everybody wants to come in.

As in solving bridge problems, or for that matter IQ tests, it is better to start from the end and work backwards. There are three ways of declaring at hi-lo at the end of the deal; simultaneously, everyone showing together by displaying coins or chips concealed in each player's fist; consecutively, by the high man on the table or the last bettor speaking first; or by letting the cards speak.

Speaking with the authority of long experience, Pug Pearson has no doubt that the third method is the proper way. "When you play hi-lo split the pot, you *gotta* play the best hand wins." Suppose you hold a goodish hand, like aces up for high and an eight for low, and one hand out against you looks like a possible flush and another hand shows low cards; Pug argues that you don't know where you are: "You've won the whole pot, but if you play declarin', why, you're up against a guess!"

Well, that's poker isn't it? Sure it's poker, but not if you're sitting with strangers. The chances of collusion are too great. The man with the four flush and the man with the possible low can signal each other if they've got it or not, and together they can whipsaw the third player out of his aces up and eight

TABLE VI
LOWBALL ODDS

Draw

			*Excluding straights and flushes, ace counts low**
Drawing one card odds against making a	10 low	even money
”	”	9	1.4–1
”	”	8	2–1
”	”	7	3–1
”	”	6	5–1
Drawing two cards	”	10 low	2–1
”	”	9	3.5–1
”	”	8	6–1
”	”	7	10–1
”	”	6	22–1
Drawing three cards	”	8 low	12–1
”	”	7	24–1
”	”	6	62–1

* If ace counts high, read the odds for the next figure down. For example, odds against making a 10-low drawing one card would be 1.4–1.

Seven Card Low

	Cards to come	Odds against making a 7 low in seven cards (excluding straights and flushes)	Odds against making an 8 low	Odds against making a 9 low
Holding three cards to the 7	4	2–1	even money	3–5
” ” ” ” ” ”	3	9–1	2–1	4–5
” ” ” ” ” ”	2	10–1	6–1	3.5–1
Holding four cards to the 7	3	12–17	2–5	1–4
” ” ” ” ” ”	2	7–5	3–4	1–2
” ” ” ” ” ”	1	3–1	2–1	4–3

low. Whereas if the cards speak, that takes care of the problem. "Declarin' is all right if you're sittin' down with six other guys and they're all gamblin'," Puggy says. "But if three of those guys ain't gamblin', you're gonna be skinned." That's a fair warning. But assuming the game is straight and among friends, declaring the hands either with coins or verbally provides an additional element of skill and suspense. The way the hands are finally shown down determines whether you try to show strength or weakness, whether you jump in to declare first or maneuver to call last.

Let's take the kind of situation Puggy gave, with three players left in the pot after the final hole card.

A (? ?) 3 ♠ 8 ♠ K ♠ Q ♥ (?)
B (? ?) 5 ♥ 9 ♠ 7 ♦ 10 ♦ (?)
C (A ♥ 4 ♠) A ♣ 2 ♦ 6 ♥ 8 ♥ (4 ♦)

What is your problem as C? The answer: You don't know if you can take the low with your 8-6 against B with his possible 7, and you don't know if you can take the high with aces up against A with his possible flush. You could beat one or the other for half the pot, which would be gratifying, but you might beat both for the whole pot, which would be doubly gratifying. Remember, though, that the normal rule is if you call hi-lo, you have to win both ways. Winning one and losing, or even tying, the other, means you lose the lot.

Cards Speak. If the hands are going to be shown up at the end, with the best cards dividing the pot, you are not in much danger. You will probably take half the pot one way or the other, and you can bet strongly. Whereas if you check, neither A nor B will bet unless they have something to see you with.

Consecutive Declaration (from the high card or last bettor). The advantage of calling last is that after the others have declared, the final player knows what he is up against, and with only three players in the pot, he may often find himself in the happy position that both the others have called the same way so that he can simply call the opposite way for a sure half of the pot.

In this hand, you might well want to speak last. Then you can cull as much information as possible to decide your own declaration, not only from the others' betting, but from the confidence or hesitation they may show in declaring, and the risks measured against money on the table. With this tactic, you would try to prompt or maneuver one of the others to take the lead.

On the other hand, look at the problem from their point of view. The flusher, if he's busted, might want to bet his hand to give the impression of strength; or would it look more convincing to check and raise?

The low hand would probably throw his cards in with a nine, but if he has a bad eight, what then? He too might see an advantage in betting out in order to declare first, lay his low on the line, and discourage you from calling the same way. With a seven low, he would presumably approach the problem the other way around, to try to persuade you to call. This is why counting out the low cards that have shown is so important. Anyone who can remember all the low cards that have fallen has some useful clues when it comes to identifying opponents' hole cards.

Simultaneous Declaration (with coins or chips in the hand). In this case you have to take a view in advance; do you go high or low or both ways? To get the answer, you certainly have to bet out aggressively.

If A calls, it probably means he is trying to back in for the high, without his flush, because he thinks both B and C are automatically going low. If A raises, he must be respected, even though it could still be a brave bluff for the high.

What about the low? You've bet, A has only called, and B comes in. That looks weak. For even with a 9-7, the call in last position is probably cheap enough. And in such a case you might well consider calling hi-lo and the hell with it. If you never take a chance when things look in your favor, you'll never be a winner.

However, if B raises instead of simply calling, it would appear that he has you beaten for low, with a 7-5, though this would require three perfect hole cards.

You have what might be termed a kind of negative protection. You know that he knows that you could, just conceivably, be low to a six, so he can't push his low regardless. On the other hand, to carry it one stage further, he knows that you know that he knows this, and therefore he could, conceivably, do just that, as if he really had you locked.

Let's leave aside the wilder possibilities . . . that the flusher, who you thought was a certain high, in fact hit an 8-4 low; or that the other man, who looked like the rival for low, has an eight and a six hidden down there for a straight; or that someone is working with a completely concealed full house. These things just don't happen, do they? Oh, is that so.

Well, who said hi-lo was an easy game.

Five card draw hi-lo is a tough little game because it's so often impossible to divine which way your opponents are going. A one card draw is usually to a low hand, statistically speaking, but it can frequently be to a straight or a flush or to two pairs. The only sound advice on what to come in on is low hands that will become virtually a sure winner on a one card draw, and high hands if you can get in cheaply.

If it comes down to just one other man in the pot, it's tempting to call the final bet whatever you hold because you have a 50-50 chance of splitting the pot. But in a game where you can call both ways on the same hand, that is, 3-4-5-6-7 or A-2-4-8-10 in suit can be both high and low, you can run into trouble chasing your ante. Occasions sometimes arise when you may go low on trips or high without a pair. For example, you draw one card to three deuces and fail to improve; your opponent draws two cards and bets strongly; the evidence suggests that he's high. You must call low; and if you've read it wrongly, hard luck.

Some games have a convention that when it comes down to just two players at the end of a hi-lo pot, one man can make an offer to split it with the other without a showdown. If the offer is accepted, they simply divide the pot without a contest. If the offer is refused, betting and declaration go on in the normal way. Splitting the pot is a bad practice. For one thing, if it happens regularly, a third player can be deliberately driven out by strong betting by two others intent on offering a split. For another thing, the man who makes the offer to split the pot has, as a rule, revealed the weakness of his hand.

All's fair in love and poker, however, and even in offering to split, a distinct element of bluff can apply. For instance, a man sitting on what seems to be a clear winner may suggest a split to lure the second player, taking his offer as a sign of weakness, to contest it. The latter then goes the "wrong" way and loses the whole pot. Well, he could've accepted the offer in the first place if he hadn't been greedy.

An emasculated version of draw hi-lo is jacks back. If no one opens for a jackpot, the betting goes around a second time for a lowball hand. What do you do if you're sitting on A-A-2-3-4? It depends on your mood whether you open for high or take your chances to go for the wheel.

The great thing about *five card stud hi-lo* (better with a twist at the end) is that there are so many opportunities to change direction in mid-hand and pull off a coup. Low cards are far the best starters, of course, but you still have all kinds of chances on middling cards if you catch a pair. Keeping the initiative is the key (see hi-lo bluff in Chapter One).

Seven card stud hi-lo is a bigger game because of the extra betting intervals, but it is in some ways easier to read. It is

also a truer game because you are not so continually depend-
ent on the luck of the last card to make or break your hand as
in five card stud hi-lo. Going for low is correct strategy, for
the obvious reason that bad cards can sometimes build up into
a high hand, but opening standards shouldn't be too rigid: just
a shade tighter than the general run in the particular game in
which you're playing.

The ideal starters are three cards to a six or a seven, but one
off card may not be too damaging if it's hidden; a lowish three
straight can also be strong or a three flush with an ace.

But you should be prepared to give any pair a run if the
matching cards are not showing, especially a low pair in the
hole, or a holding like (5-2)-5-2, because the opposition will
certainly read you for low, and you will be able to sock it to
them with a vengeance if you fill.

Above all, it is essential to count the low cards. There are
times when you can not only be certain what a rival can't
have, but can be certain he can't improve. If you are holding
a 6-4 low against a very powerful-looking five, and you happen
to know where all the deuces are, you may have your unsus-
pecting opponent locked. If you know where only three of the
deuces are, you will still get a better reading on what he may
have in the hole.

To take the reverse point, on occasion a full house may go
low. Here is an example from play. Showing K-6-K-8 and
with the comfortable feeling that you get from having another
king and a six in the hole to make a full house, one of the
better players in the game found himself in a big pot against a
man betting on (?-?)-7-8-7-J off suit with every sign of confidence.

After the last card down, the pair of sevens raised back into
him. Why? The kings were clearly marked as a higher hand
by the pattern of betting; alternatively, if the raiser was being
"clever" with a concealed 8-7 low, he was still at risk of being

clipped by an 8-6. The two-kings man couldn't remember seeing any sevens out and decided, since it looked obvious that he must have a full house himself to have come so far, that there must be four of a kind against him. He declared low and saved a large loss.

Wild cards at poker are a matter of choice, but certain varieties have become established. *Baseball* is one of the liveliest, a form of seven card stud with threes (three strikes) and nines (nine innings) wild, with the additional quirk that if a player receives a four (four balls) face up, he gets an extra card down. Moreover, although it's a wild card, anyone who catches a red three showing faces the penalty of doubling the size of the pot. That is such an overwhelming liability for a wild card that any game I've ever played in has reduced it to a fixed charge, say 5 or 10 chips.

Baseball is a fast-and-loose game, just right for hometown poker. With eight wild cards, plus the extra cards coming because of the fours, everyone has chances to make a hand. In practice, without at least one wild card in the hole plus either an ace or two cards to a straight flush, you're better off chucking in, because someone else is probably starting with two jokers, minimum. As for a red three, you need to be virtually certain of winning if you're going to pay for the privilege. Fours of a kind are cheap, straight flushes pretty good, and fives sometimes appear, which in most games rank above even a royal straight flush.

I've even played baseball hi-lo, but there are too many wild cards running around to make a serious contest of it.

Other variations of seven card stud with wild cards which have their own brand names include *Woolworth's* (fives and tens wild), *Betty Hutton* (fives and nines), and *Dr. Pepper* (twos, fours, and tens). . . . Yeah, you're quite right about that.

Summing it all up, there are three ways in which poker hands can be varied; any permutation of them can be used to devise new games.

So far as the *deal* is concerned, which is the first major variable, players can have any number of cards from two up to, say, ten, though the final hand declared has got to be ranked in poker terms, which normally means five cards; the cards can be dealt up, down, or in common to all players in the hand. Secondly, coming to the actual *play* of the hand, the cards dealt may be kept down, rolled face up, exchanged in the draw, or even passed to another player. Finally, the *values* of the cards themselves may be changed either by designating new hands, for instance, ranking a four flush above one pair, or by assigning some cards as jokers.

There are sufficient alternatives here to make the varieties of poker, if not infinite, at least very large.

If ever a poker game appears to be exhausted, only a minor change is required to give it a new lease on life. In practice, poker will never be exhausted (as theoretically chess might begin to be if opening theory were mastered to such an extent that good players knew all the opening lines twenty-five moves deep) because poker does not depend on the ingenuity of its rules. Poker is preeminently a game of character, and so long as you can find five or six fellows who want to sit down and play cards, you will have a new game going, represented by the interplay of their personalities.

The idea of other games beyond the five and seven card versions is to achieve variety.

Here are three hybrids to be recommended and three to be avoided. To be commended, as one example, is a game known as *Sweeney Todd* or *Fiery cross* and doubtless answering to many other names. After each player is dealt a regular hand of five cards as in draw, five cards are dealt face down in the middle as community cards; they are turned up one by one with a betting round after each new card is shown.

It's a good hi-lo game, though sometimes funny things can happen. But as in all poker variations, the basic principles still apply, which insure that the better players win. In the fiery cross version of this game, each player gets four cards down and five cards are laid out in the middle in the shape of a cross. You can use either the upright or the crossbar cards, that is, three cards to make your hand, with the one in the middle, which fits in both lines of the cross, turned up last.

Playing for low, you can feel safe only by going for the wheel, which in effect means starting with four low cards; if all high cards show in the middle, you can treat your hand as you would in draw lowball and take an eight or nine pat low as pretty strong; but if low cards appear, you can be sure other players will be making use of them too. Thus, even with a wheel, you may tie for low, which would mean dividing the low half of the pot again with the other low winner. With three players at the showdown, one of whom calls high, you are contributing .3 of the pot for a dividend of .25 as opposed to the normal .5. This is a risk that is common to any hi-lo game where the number of cards dealt, or more probably the addition of wild cards, makes the wheel relatively easy to hit. Going for high, a pair of aces with an ace in the middle is strong and worth betting all the way through, and by the same token any high trips are extremely playable; but once a higher card appears in the middle, beware. If a pair shows, even deuces, someone else has probably hit a full already, and the possibility of fours is risky; in such a case, a deuce in your own hand is an extremely useful defensive card.

Another variation to be recommended is the geed up version of five card stud hi-lo known affectionately as *Screw your buddy*. Each player has the option of taking each successive up card as it is dealt or passing it on to the next player on his left, who then has the same choice; if you pass the card, you have to keep the next one dealt. Some of the financial journalists in Washington dubbed this game *Crawling peg*, after one of the more intricate devices of international monetary theory.

It's an ingenious game, with numerous opportunities for bluff. Sitting on low cards, you naturally pass on anything higher than a seven or an eight. But suppose you are sitting over another player going low. Do you pass him a low card you don't need or do you screw him? For example, you have (5)-6-8 and catch another five. No use giving it to him with (?)-4-7, so you keep the five and let him take the next card, hoping it may be high. Meanwhile, despite the pair, you still look like going for low, and can bet your hand. Or suppose your (5)-6-8 is beaten in sight by a better low, and a king or a queen comes around the board. If you keep it, everyone is going to read you for the pair. It's a game where chances abound for staging a coup.

Roll your own, when each player decides which card to roll face up and which to keep down in the hole, also gives plenty of scope for imagination and bluff. It can be applied to five or seven card stud hi-lo, the latter being particularly lethal because it becomes so easy to keep full houses concealed. With a full house you can show (7-4)-2-3-4-7-(7) and look very low; with a low hand building, you can show (A-2)-3-K-K-4 with a lock to draw to. It is, all the same, a very accurate game.

Not to be recommended are games where you have to win the pot twice to win. That is, the first pot, whether you win it without being seen or by beating the others outright, remains intact on the table; the game, whatever choice it is, proceeds to a second deal, and someone else may win that hand, in which case the pot goes on building, and that player is also in with a chance; there is no winner until someone wins it twice.

The point of this elaborate exercise is that it builds up a monstrous pot, but poker values are totally distorted in the process. The same objection goes for having two draws at a hand, in, say, draw hi-lo. The game gets out of proportion.

Points count is another dodgy one. The idea here is to score the pips on the cards. Let's say aces count as 1 or 11; the best low hand would be 6 points—A-A-A-A-2—and the best high hand would be that nearest to 54 points—A-A-A-A with a K, Q, J or 10. Poker values do apply, in a way, but what's really happening is that the deck is being revamped so as to invert the normal scale of hands; instead of the wheel, the best low is four aces; instead of a straight flush, a pair of aces and three court cards are unbeatable. Who needs it?

Another variation to be avoided is hi-lo in which, say, the lowest spade in the hole counts automatically as the best low hand, or variations on that theme. It's simply paying a high premium for the ace of spades to be dealt face down, allowing the lucky player who gets it to bet his heart out, and the man with 2 spades to go broke. It distorts normal values too grossly. Making the low card in the hole wild at seven card stud has rather more to it, but not much. You may have a strong hand at the start with, say, (5-5) in the hole, then find that the last card ruins you because it's a four. It's simply too chancy a game to appeal to serious players.

If one is looking for hard-luck stories on the turn of a card at hi-lo, here's one to end up on. Claudio was one of the best players in London, in his day, that is, one of those ageless, heavy-eyed Greek gentlemen, meticulously polite at the table, forever sucking on an empty cigarette holder as he played his cards. Draw was his specialty; he had a way of suspecting, or "sussing out," as the cockney expression has it, what you held in your hand even before you knew yourself how strong it might be.

He was not in the same league at hi-lo, though still pretty adept, and one of the occasions when lightning struck, which he never quite forgot or forgave, concerned a hand in one of the games described above, Sweeney.

Claudio was dealt A-A-A-5-6 in his hand, which is extremely good, if not indeed sensational, because it needs only a five or a six or any pair out of the five community cards shown up in the middle to make the best full house, and he also has good possibilities for low. First card to show was a three, which Claudio bet on, as the chance of a six low was now very high. Even better, the next card was the ace of spades, giving him four of a kind. At that point he eased up to let all the others come in. Third and fourth cards were a king and a queen and changed nothing, so Claudio came back in with a modest bet, to encourage everyone to put their money in. The last card to show looked innocuous enough, the 2 ♠.

In the middle, 3 ♥ A ♠ K ♣ Q ♦ 2 ♠; in his own hand, A ♣ A ♦ A ♥ 5 ♣ 6 ♠. Declaration was by cards speak. The four aces were solid and there was a strong chance that the 6-5 would take the low too. What could possibly go wrong?

But alas and alack, the 2 ♠ proved fatal, and will no doubt be engraved on Claudio's tombstone. One man who had been hanging on, perhaps imprudently, with a six and a four in his hand, caught an unbeatable six low; and someone else, who had been trying to sneak in for low with 3 ♠ 4 ♠ 5♠ in his hand, suddenly saw to his total surprise that the A ♠ and the 2 ♠ on the table gave him a straight flush. Any other card than the 2 ♠, according to Claudio, would have netted him over £6,000. Instead of which he lost two grand. Which only goes to show that sometimes the odds will buck around and wallop you on the nose.

Index